CONTROVERSIES

The Industrial
Food Complex

Other Books in the Current Controversies Series

The Industrial
Food Complex

Joellen McCarty, Book Editor

GREENHAVEN
PUBLISHING

Published in 2020 by Greenhaven Publishing, LLC
353 3rd Avenue, Suite 255, New York, NY 10010

Articles in Greenhaven Publishing anthologies are often edited for length to meet page
requirements. In addition, original titles of these works are changed to clearly present
the main thesis and to explicitly indicate the author's opinion. Every effort is made to
ensure that Greenhaven Publishing accurately reflects the original intent of the authors.
Every effort has been made to trace the owners of the copyrighted material.

Cover image: I Love Coffee dot Today/Shutterstock.com

Library of Congress Cataloging-in-Publication Data

Names: McCarty, Joellen, editor.
Title: The industrial food complex / Joellen McCarty, book editor.
Other titles: Current controversies.
Description: First edition. | New York, NY : Greenhaven Publishing, LLC,
  2020. | Series: Current controversies | Includes bibliographical
  references and index. | Audience: Grades 9–12.
Identifiers: LCCN 2019003302| ISBN 9781534505391 (library bound) | ISBN
  9781534505407 (pbk.)
Subjects: LCSH: Food industry and trade—Health aspects. | Food industry and
  trade—Environmental aspects. | Food industry and trade—Economic aspects.
Classification: LCC HD9000.5 .I5415 2020 | DDC 338.4/7664—dc23
LC record available at https://lccn.loc.gov/2019003302

Manufactured in the United States of America

Website: http://greenhavenpublishing.com

Contents

Chapter 1: Does the Industrial Food Complex Present a Public Health Problem?

David Wallinga

The industrialization of agriculture has had a myriad of effects on food production, food retail, the creation of monocultures, and the use of pesticides on farms. Agribusiness offers food at lower prices, but there may be hidden health and environmental costs.

Yes: The Industrial Food Complex Is a Public Health Problem

John Ikerd

Industrial agriculture is inherently unsustainable. Agribusiness relies on fossil fuels, fosters nutrition-related deficiencies such as obesity, and does not provide for the needs of developing countries.

Kumi Naidoo

Agribusiness uses homogenous farming techniques and monocultures, permanently depleting soil resources and contributing immensely to climate change. This, in turn, results in inadequate food supply and contributes to global hunger.

No: The Industrial Food Complex Is Not a Public Health Problem

Ramez Naam

Agribusiness funds the creation and development of GMOs. GMOs can help large-scale farms embrace organic farming and decrease their effect on the environment.

While food production and the byproducts that result from it can create a large amount of waste and have negative environmental impacts, industrial agriculture has the opportunity to be at the forefront of efforts to reuse byproducts, which would help reduce hunger and waste.

Chapter 2: Does the Industrial Food Complex Encourage Obesity?

Obesity rates in the United States have been increasing for a century. Key contributors to obesity's rise include increased daily calorie intake, a "toxic" food environment, and a lack of exercise.

Yes: The Industrial Food Complex Encourages Obesity

Agribusiness has created an environment in which obesity is normal by offering primarily sugar-laden, fatty, industrially produced food. Although this food is addictive, agribusiness shifts blame for obesity onto consumers instead of self-regulating.

Increased average portion sizes directly correlate to obesity rates in the United States. Despite USDA guidelines, agribusiness continues to promote oversize food portions.

Chapter 4: Does the Industrial Food Complex Increase Economic Inequality?

Yes: The Industrial Food Complex Increases Income Inequality

Foreword

Controversy is a word that has an undeniably unpleasant connotation. It carries a definite negative charge. Controversy can spoil family gatherings, spread a chill around classroom and campus discussion, inflame public discourse, open raw civic wounds, and lead to the ouster of public officials. We often feel that controversy is almost akin to bad manners, a rude and shocking eruption of that which must not be spoken or thought of in polite, tightly guarded society. To avoid controversy, to quell controversy, is often seen as a public good, a victory for etiquette, perhaps even a moral or ethical imperative.

Yet the studious, deliberate avoidance of controversy is also a whitewashing, a denial, a death threat to democracy. It is a false sterilizing and sanitizing and superficial ordering of the messy, ragged, chaotic, at times ugly processes by which a healthy democracy identifies and confronts challenges, engages in passionate debate about appropriate approaches and solutions, and arrives at something like a consensus and a broadly accepted and supported way forward. Controversy is the megaphone, the speaker's corner, the public square through which the citizenry finds and uses its voice. Controversy is the life's blood of our democracy and absolutely essential to the vibrant health of our society.

Our present age is certainly no stranger to controversy. We are consumed by fierce debates about technology, privacy, political correctness, poverty, violence, crime and policing, guns, immigration, civil and human rights, terrorism, militarism, environmental protection, and gender and racial equality. Loudly competing voices are raised every day, shouting opposing opinions, putting forth competing agendas, and summoning starkly different visions of a utopian or dystopian future. Often these voices attempt to shout the others down; there is precious little listening and considering among the cacophonous din. Yet listening and considering, too, are essential to the health of a democracy. If controversy is democracy's lusty lifeblood, respectful listening and careful thought are its higher faculties, its brain, its conscience.

Current Controversies does not shy away from or attempt to hush the loudly competing voices. It seeks to provide readers with as wide and representative as possible a range of articulate voices on any given controversy of the day, separates each one out to allow it to be heard clearly and fairly, and encourages careful listening to each of these well-crafted, thoughtfully expressed opinions, supplied by some of today's leading academics, thinkers, analysts, politicians, policy makers, economists, activists, change agents, and advocates. Only after listening to a wide range of opinions on an issue, evaluating the strengths and weaknesses of each argument, assessing how well the facts and available evidence mesh with the stated opinions and conclusions, and thoughtfully and critically examining one's own beliefs and conscience can the reader begin to arrive at his or her own conclusions and articulate his or her own stance on the spotlighted controversy.

This process is facilitated and supported in each Current Controversies volume by an introduction and chapter overviews that provide readers with the essential context they need to begin engaging with the spotlighted controversies, with the debates surrounding them, and with their own perhaps shifting or nascent opinions on them. Chapters are organized around several key questions that are answered with diverse opinions representing all points on the political spectrum. In its content, organization, and methodology, readers are encouraged to determine the authors' point of view and purpose, interrogate and analyze the various arguments and their rhetoric and structure, evaluate the arguments' strengths and weaknesses, test their claims against available facts and evidence, judge the validity of the reasoning, and bring into clearer, sharper focus the reader's own beliefs and conclusions and how they may differ from or align with those in the collection or those of classmates.

Research has shown that reading comprehension skills improve dramatically when students are provided with compelling, intriguing, and relevant "discussable" texts. The subject matter of these collections could not be more compelling, intriguing, or urgently relevant to today's students and the world they are poised to inherit. The anthologized articles also provide the basis for stimulating, lively, and passionate classroom debates. Students who are compelled to anticipate objections to their own argument and identify the flaws in those of an opponent read more carefully, think more critically, and steep themselves in relevant context, facts, and information more thoroughly. In short, using discussable text of the kind provided by every single volume in the Current Controversies series encourages close reading, facilitates reading comprehension, fosters research, strengthens critical thinking, and greatly enlivens and energizes classroom discussion and participation. The entire learning process is deepened, extended, and strengthened.

If we are to foster a knowledgeable, responsible, active, and engaged citizenry, we must provide readers with the intellectual, interpretive, and critical-thinking tools and experience necessary to make sense of the world around them and of the all-important debates and arguments that inform it. We must encourage them not to run away from or attempt to quell controversy but to embrace it in a responsible, conscientious, and thoughtful way, to sharpen and strengthen their own informed opinions by listening to and critically analyzing those of others. This series encourages respectful engagement with and analysis of current controversies and competing opinions and fosters a resulting increase in the strength and rigor of one's own opinions and stances. As such, it helps readers assume their rightful place in the public square and provides them with the skills necessary to uphold their awesome responsibility—guaranteeing the continued and future health of a vital, vibrant, and free democracy.

Introduction

> "The question of what to have for dinner assails every omnivore, and always has. When you can eat just about anything nature has to offer, deciding what you should eat will inevitably stir anxiety."
>
> - Michael Pollan, American journalist and activist[1]

For many in the United States, deciding what to eat is no longer just a matter of survival; what one eats links back to diet concerns, debates over the role of businesses and governments, political stances, the power of the individual to create change, and, unavoidably, the complicated system known as the industrial food complex. The industrial food complex encompasses a global network of businesses that produce and supply most of the world's food. The complex includes agriculture, manufacturing, food processing, advertising and marketing, food distribution, food service, as well as research and food lobbying. The simple act of deciding what to cook for dinner puts each of us in contact with the industrial food complex.

Industrialization drastically changed the way the United States interacts with food. Since the 1950s, the farm system has rapidly industrialized.[2] The old methods of family farming—farms run by individuals or families growing a variety of crops for personal and public use, including feed for animals—were replaced by industrial farms. An industrial farm is owned by a corporation rather than a family, and as industries grew, industrial farms laid claim to more and more land. Industrial farms drastically increased production scales not only through land use, but also by focusing on one or two products instead of a myriad. This method of farming is known as a monoculture. In particular, large industrial farms often focus on corn, which is cheap to grow and used for a variety of purposes. Corn is harvested and turned into products such as corn syrup, and it is also used as a replacement for traditional animal feed. By using fossil fuels and pesticides, industrialized farms are able to produce a much larger volume of products at cheaper prices, which translates into less expensive food for the average consumer. Today, in parts of the Midwestern United States, 90 percent of farmland is used for corn or soybeans.[3] As corn flourishes, so does the industry surrounding it, creating new technological innovations such as genetically modified crops.

The industrial food complex may begin with farms, but it doesn't end with them—the complex includes producers, suppliers, advertisers, and retailers—concluding with the food found in grocery stores or restaurants. However, politicians, farmers, activists, scholars, and consumers are concerned with the possible hidden costs of the industrial food complex. One possible hidden cost is the environmental impact. Industrial farms and agribusiness generally rely on fossil fuels and pesticides in order to maintain their production and planting cycles. Agribusiness is linked to deforestation, air pollution, and water pollution.

Another possible hidden cost is to public health. Any severe ecological cost will take its toll on the human population as well. Some argue that the environmental unsustainability of industrial agriculture places food security at risk.[4] Agribusiness, critics argue, depletes natural resources to the extent that once-farmable land is now barren.[5] The fertilizers factory farms use pollute the water supply, damaging one necessary ingredient for food growth. Further public health risks include nutrition-related diseases. In 2018, the Centers for Disease Control and Prevention (CDC) reported that the obesity rate was at 39.8%, affecting nearly 93.3 million adults in the United States.[6] Many link unhealthy food options—provided cheaply and often by agribusiness—to growing obesity rates.[7]

A final consideration is the industrial food complex's relationship to economic inequality. It has been perceived alternately as both increasing and decreasing economic inequality. Providing food at low costs means more people can afford to sustain themselves, and the industrial food complex creates jobs in many areas and on various levels, both skilled and unskilled. However, industrial farms replace family farms, which have become increasingly less common since the 1950s.[8] There are concerns over low wages in the fast food industry and for farm workers around the world, as well as over the availability of healthy food options in low-income communities.

At the heart of these debates is a larger discussion: How does and how should the government, businesses, and consumers mediate one another? Are businesses responsible for—and ultimately invested in—the public good? Are consumers responsible on an individual level for what they eat, and are they responsible for demanding that businesses make more sustainable choices? How should the government mediate disputes between agribusiness and smaller farms, as well as those regarding agribusiness's impact on the environment?

Eating is non-negotiable. However, what we eat, why we eat, and what we should be eating is up for debate. Throughout *Current Controversies: The Industrial Food Complex*, environmental activists, journalists, policy experts, and scholars will discuss and debate these key questions.

Notes

1. *The Omnivore's Dilemma*, Michael Pollan, pg. 4.

2. "Today's Food System: How Healthy Is It?" David Wallinga, https://www.ncbi.nlm .nih.gov/pmc/articles/PMC3489133/.

3. "Today's Food System: How Healthy Is It?" David Wallinga, https://www.ncbi.nlm .nih.gov/pmc/articles/PMC3489133/.

4. "Can Industrial Agriculture Provide Global Food Security?" John Ikerd, http:// web.missouri.edu/ikerdj/papers/California%20-%20IPDC%20-%20Small%20 Farms.htm.

5. "Pollution (Water, Air, Chemicals)," Food is Power, http://www.foodispower.org/pollution-water-air-chemicals/.

6. "Adult Obesity Facts," CDC, https://www.cdc.gov/obesity/data/adult.html.

7. "Inside the Food Industry: The Surprising Truth about What You Eat," Joanna Blythman, *The Guardian*, https://www.theguardian.com/lifeandstyle/2015/feb/21/a-feast-of-engineering-whats-really-in-your-food.

8. "Today's Food System: How Healthy Is It?" David Wallinga, https://www.ncbi.nlm.nih.gov/pmc/articles/PMC3489133/.

CHAPTER 1

Does the Industrial Food Complex Present a Public Health Problem?

Industrial Agriculture Has Fundamentally Changed the Way the US Food System Functions

David Wallinga is a senior health advisor for the Natural Resources Defense Council (NRDC), a nonprofit environmental advocacy organization. He holds a bachelor's degree in political science from Dartmouth College, a master's degree in public affairs from Princeton University, and completed medical school at the University of Minnesota.

[…]

Prior to the late 1950s, farms in the upper Midwest, the American "Corn Belt," grew row crops like corn and soybeans but only on about half the farmland, where it was interspersed with other small grains, hay, and pasture. Grain, hay, and pasture on the farm typically were not commoditized or sold but were fed to one or more kinds of animals on the same farm.[1] It was a type of food production system where the farming and the health of the ecosystem were closely linked and environmental degradation was uncommon, as Altieri and Nicholls[2] have described:

> [C]rop yields in agricultural systems depended on internal resources, recycling of organic matter, built-in biological control mechanisms and rainfall patterns. Agricultural yields were modest, but stable. Production was safeguarded by growing more than one crop or variety in space and time in a field as insurance against pest outbreaks or severe weather. Inputs of nitrogen were gained by rotating major field crops with legumes. In turn rotations suppressed insects, weeds and diseases by effectively breaking the life cycles of these pests (p. 13).

David Wallinga, "Today's Food System: How Healthy Is It?" *Journal of Hunger & Environmental Nutrition*, Taylor & Francis Group, December 11, 2009.

The farm family lived there on the farm and performed most of the labor themselves with little or no hired help or specialized machinery.[2] They too were an integral part of the agro-ecosystem; their health and well-being were intimately tied to it. That typical integrated Midwestern farm of a few decades ago is well on its way to extinction.

What Is Meant by Industrialization?

Over the last 150 years, industrialization slowly transformed American agriculture, including the mindset of farmers. New technologies have been one important driver of industrialization: the advent of cheap, abundant fossil fuels; the innovation of new higher-yielding plant and animal breeds; farm mechanization; and changes in railroads, highways, and other transportation infrastructure, as well as in refrigeration, making it easier to ship agricultural products to distant points. Industrialization has transformed American agriculture from a local, smaller-scale enterprise where most of the needs of the farm were met by on-farm resources into a much more specialized enterprise, one consolidated into ever fewer and more massive farms, where off-farm resources such as fossil fuel energy, pesticides, and fertilizers are used intensively. Specialization means that whereas the typical American farm once produced many different things (e.g., corn, oats, wheat, chickens, hogs, cows, milk, etc.), including both crops and animals, it now produces just one or two commodities, and crop production has been "delinked" from the raising of food animals to which most grains and other grasses on the farm used to be fed.

The specialization, scale, and resource intensiveness of industrialized agriculture all impact on human and ecosystem health in ways that are best appreciated from a systems perspective. For example, the delinking of crop from animal production has rendered infeasible a number of practices that historically provided important services adding to the health and resilience of the food production system. Rotation of corn with soybeans or other nitrogen-fixing crops helped replenish soil nitrogen; the growing of multiple crops ("multicropping") also helped to suppress the lifecycles of pests and disease.[2] Animals once provided cheap horsepower for crop production, and animal manure plus crop refuse (corn stover, etc.) in turn was recycled to restore organic matter and fertility into soil as part of a low-cost, closed-loop system. Soils high in organic content can sequester more carbon, better resist erosion, and help retain more rainwater, making them more resilient during drought. Indirect impacts of the loss of these ecosystem functions on human health are discussed in the following section.

Over the last 5 decades especially, the changes begun under the initial industrialization of agricultural crystallized into what Lang and Heasman have termed a *productionist* mindset—placing short-term quantity or yield over all other priorities. This has become the dominant 20th-century outlook for the food system not only in the United States but globally.[3]

What Does Agricultural Industrialization Look Like?

Under industrialized or productionist agriculture, rural farm landscapes have transformed in appearance; once diverse landscapes, agro-ecosystems comprised of mixtures of crops, animals, pastures and woodlots, have given way to "monocultures"—ever-larger homogeneous farms, specializing in a single commodity. In ecological and economic terms as well, this transformation has been dramatic. In some counties in the heart of the Corn Belt over 90% of farmland is planted in corn or soybeans[1] and increasingly in just corn. Moderately sized Iowa farms (100 to 500 acres) are disappearing;[4] of the farms that remain, 60% are larger than 1000 acres.[1]

Economies of scale in the production of single commodities, or monocultures, helped precipitate the trend toward larger farms, with more acres under till.[1] Ever larger machinery meant that greater acreage in corn and soybeans could be planted and then harvested in very narrow calendar windows, sparing labor.[5] Specially designed seed varieties plus the use of insecticides made it possible in the short term to grow only corn, year after year, without significant yield consequences. Herbicide-tolerant soybean breeds also have reduced the summer hours previously needed to "walk the beans" for the control of weeds.

Since Corn Belt farms are increasingly devoted to monocultures of single crops, crop farmers have no animals to tend, and the help of machinery, fuels, and new seeds means less time than ever is required to plant, weed, and harvest their huge acreage. As a result, today's crop farmer has few reasons to be on the farm for most of the year. Second jobs are typical. From within the industrial agricultural economic model, these changes typically are perceived as gains in efficiency.

Bigger machines and chemical-intensive production [have] made farming much more capital intensive, however. An estimated half a million dollars in capital are required to support a farm today, raising a significant economic barrier for the entry of new farmers.[6] With more than 60% of farm operators 55 years of age or older in 1997, this looms as an important issue.

In addition, because crop farmers are now delinked from the animal-related fertilizer and recycling practices that previously added health and resilience to on-farm systems, they have turned instead to off-farm resources or "inputs." Along with specialization, the intensive use of these inputs is a hallmark of industrialized production. Moving from horses or oxen to mechanized tractors, farmers traded farm "tools" that could be fed on forage to ones fed only on fossil fuels. Crop monocultures, made possible by the use of hybrid seed varieties fertilized with inorganic off-farm, natural gas-derived fertilizers, have replaced diverse multicropping systems that were fertilized by on-farm manure or other organic residues. Crop monocultures, however, also encourage pest outbreaks by concentrating the opportunities for pests (rodent, insect, and weed) of these crops to thrive while also undermining the integrated ecosystems that might play host to the natural enemies of these pests.[6] The new plant hybrids, like "Roundup Ready" corn or soybeans, therefore have been specially designed to tolerate heavy applications of herbicides without being killed themselves. The patented seeds, which must be purchased annually from off-farm, in some cases replace seeds collected on-farm for free by the farmer. The herbicides too are derived from off-farm petroleum.

Movement of animals off-farm has made the on-farm use of organic manure impractical or uneconomic or both. What has been lost is more than just an inexpensive, on-farm source of fertility. Over the past few decades, crop farmers who had animal barns or fences remaining on their property came to see them as unproductive assets and got rid of them. Now, nondiversified crop farmers can no longer "hedge their bets" when grain crops fail or the prices are low, by raising and selling animal products— their production model is more vulnerable by virtue of its lack of diversification. As will be discussed, public policy has encouraged this transformation.

Moving the discussion from crop to food animal production, the increased specialization in industrialized agriculture also has meant that animal operations focus on producing just one species, and increasingly, one age range for that animal; for example, facilities devoted to only small, "weaner" pigs that are later shipped to other facilities for maturing to slaughter size. Larger-scale production means hundreds or thousands of hogs or poultry typically are confined indoors in a single building, with many such facilities clustered spatially and often regionally. Large animal numbers mean large quantities of manure waste are generated and concentrated in these areas as well.

Off-farm resources used intensively by these industrialized animal facilities include feed grains, water and energy, as well as antibiotics and other feed additives. The poultry and hog industries are the most industrialized. The most delinked from pasture-based production, they are the systems most based on indoor confinement of animals and therefore on feeding animals a diet of feed grains rather than of crop residues or the other by-products on which animal production had previously relied. The poultry and hog industries consume over 75% of cereal and oilseed-based concentrated animal feeds, worldwide.[7] Corn and soybeans constitute 83% to 91% of these feed grains, and so 55% to 65% of the US corn crop and 45% to 50% of its soybeans are consumed by domestic livestock and poultry.[8]

Lacking the associated cropland to spread manure as fertilizer, large-scale industrial livestock producers have found few alternatives other than to waste it. The manure cannot be economically transported for any distance. It therefore is often disposed of in ways that lead to nutrient runoff and pollution of surface and/or groundwater resources. USDA data demonstrate that the largest industrial hog operations tend to be those with the most manure pollution problems; that is, where manure is disposed of as waste product rather than a productive resource.[9]

Industrialization of the food system, it is important to note, has been happening globally. Further, industrialization has occurred all along the food supply chain, as processors acquired the capacity to preserve, store, and distribute huge volumes of food. Over recent decades, these food processors grew both horizontally (by buying competitors) and vertically (by buying their own suppliers and distributors), leading to market concentration. Eventually, this growth gave rise to increasingly global trade of grains, meat, and other food products, which in turn became another driver in the further industrialization of the food system. US trade "liberalization" policies in food have had the effect of reinforcing these patterns.

Globalization of the food system has had impacts on patterns of resource use and pollution, as well as on social health.[3, 10] Power in the food system is shifting from the production end to food processors and retailers that operate globally, and this has important health implications as well.[10] For example, contractual agreements increasingly bind the financial interests of farmers to the interests of both the buyers of their output and the suppliers of their inputs.[6] By 1997, just 163,000 farms accounted for over 61%

of total American farm production, and 63% of those produced a single agricultural commodity under contract to consolidated firms, often global in nature.

[…]

Notes

1. Jackson LL. "Who 'Designs' the Agricultural Landscape?" *Landscape*. 2008; 27:1–8.

2. Altieri MA, Nicholls CI. *Agroecology and the Search for a Truly Sustainable Agriculture*, 1st ed. Available at: http://www.agroeco.org/doc/agroecology-engl-PNUMA.pdf. Accessed July 17, 2009.

3. Lang T, Heasman M. *Food Wars: The Global Battle for Mouths, Minds and Markets*. London: Earthscan; 2004.

4. Kirschenmann F, Stevenson S, Buttel F, Lyson T, Duffy M. "Why Worry About the Agriculture of the Middle?" Available at: http://www.agofthemiddle.org. Accessed July 16, 2009.

5. Ray DE. "Agricultural Policy for the Twenty-First Century and the Legacy of the Wallaces." (The Fourth Annual Pesek Colloquium Lecture) The Henry A. Wallace Endowed Chair for Sustainable Agriculture Web site. Available at: http://www.wallacechair.iastate.edu/PDF/Daryll_RAy.pdf. Accessed July 16, 2009.

6. Heller MC, Keoleian GA. "Assessing the Sustainability of the US Food System: A Life Cycle Perspective." *Agric Syst*. 2003; 76:1007–1041.

7. Galloway JN, Burke M, Bradford GE, et al. "International Trade in Meat: The Tip of the Pork Chop." *Ambio*. 2007; 36:622–629. [PubMed]

8. Wise T. "Identifying the Real Winners from US Agricultural Policies." Global Development and Environmental Institute, Tufts University Web site. Available at: http://www.ase.tufts.edu/gdae/Pubs/wp/05-07RealWinnersUSAg.pdf. Accessed July 26, 2009.

9. Ribaudo M, Gollehon N, Aillery M, et al. "Agricultural Economic Report 824: Manure Management for Water Quality: Costs to Animal Feeding Operations of Applying Manure Nutrients to Land." Available at: http://www.ers.usda.gov/Publications/AER824. Accessed July 23, 2009.

10. Lang T, Barling D, Caraher M. *Food Policy: Integrating Health, Environment and Society*. New York, NY: Oxford University Press; 2009.

Industrial Agriculture Prevents Global Food Security

John Ikerd

John Ikerd is a professor emeritus at the University of Missouri. He is the author of six books focused on sustainable agriculture and economics, including Small Farms are Real Farms: Sustaining People through Agriculture *(2007) and* Crisis and Opportunity: Sustainability in American Agriculture *(2008).*

The prevailing agricultural ideology seems to be that industrial agriculture, meaning large, specialized, mechanized farms, will be necessary to meet the food needs of a growing global population. The logic or reasoning supporting this ideology is: Global population is destined to grow from the current seven billion to at least nine billion people by the middle of this century. More people obviously will require more food. And, industrial agriculture is the only logical means of increasing global food production.

The basic flaw in this logic is that industrializing global agriculture meaning replacing the remaining small, diversified farms with large, specialized farms is *not* the only means of increasing global food production. In fact, with greater scarcity and rising costs of fossil energy and the progression of global climate change, industrial agriculture is becoming less productive and may not even survive the twenty-first century. As we have seen in recent years, the global economy has no nationality, no sense of social responsibility, or concern for the future of humanity. Nations that depend on industrial agriculture for their food security face a future of growing dependence on a few large multinational food corporations that have no allegiance to anything other than maximum profit and growth.

The blind faith in the future of industrial agriculture is based on its record of increasing productivity over the past 50 to 60 years. Admittedly, yields of crops per acre or hectare of farmland production of meat, milk, and eggs per bushel or ton of feed have increased during this period. However, virtually all of these increases have been linked directly or indirectly to an increased reliance on abundant and inexpensive fossil energy. Cheap nitrogen fertilizers were readily available because of an abundance of natural gas. Climate-controlled buildings for livestock were economically feasible because of low-cost fuel for heating and ventilation. Fossil fuels provided energy not only for traction but also for manufacturing of machinery. Deep-well irrigation likewise depends on low cost energy to pump and distribute water. Most pesticides are also fossil-energy based materials. Industrial agriculture is inherently fossil-energy dependent.

In the United States, for example, approximately 10 calories of fossil energy is required for each calorie of food energy produced.[1] About two-thirds of this total is accounted for by food processing, manufacturing, transportation, packaging and other processes of the industrial food system. But, even at the farm level, industrial agriculture requires about three kcals of fossil energy per kcal of food produced. In addition, industrial agriculture is impractical, if not impossible, without an industrial system of processing and distribution. Industrial agriculture depends on a fossil energy dependent food system.

Energy experts differ on their estimates of how much recoverable fossil energy is left to be extracted from the earth. Some experts claim that most economically recoverable fossil energy reserves will be depleted within fifty years while others believe there is enough fossil energy for another 100 to 150 years. However, there is no disagreement that the remaining reserves of fossil energy will be more difficult and costly to extract, as we are seeing with the fracking process required to extract shale gas and the costs and risks of deep-sea oil drilling. Beyond some point in each extraction process production will peak; there will be less fossil energy available each year thereafter. Each time demand increases relative to supplies, prices of fossil energy will rise and eventually will rise dramatically. An agriculture that is dependent on fossil energy quite simply is not sustainable.

With increases in fossil energy demand of 2.5% per year, which is typical of recent years, total fossil energy demand would double every 30 years. This means twice as much fossil energy would be needed by 2045, four times as much by 2075, and eight times as much by 2105. Renewable energy from wind, water, passive solar, and photovoltaic cells eventually must replace fossil energy in agriculture as well as elsewhere in the economy. But, useful energy from renewable sources will be less abundant and more expensive than the fossil energy of the past century. The era of abundant, inexpensive energy is over.

In addition, industrial agriculture places similarly unsustainable demands on fossil water, or slow-recharging aquifers, for irrigation, half of which has already been depleted by some estimates.[2,3] Other estimates indicate that the earth's mineable phosphorus reserves could be depleted in 50–100 years, with a peak occurring around 2030.[4] In addition, industrial agriculture is destroying the natural productivity of soils through erosion, salinization, and agrochemical contamination. Fertilizers and agricultural pesticides also are major contributors to pollution of groundwater, streams, and estuaries. Industrial agriculture is a major contributor to global climate change, and the related weather instability will be a major challenge to global food security in the future.[5] In summary, industrial agriculture depletes the natural resource base that supports its productivity and pollutes the natural environment that sustains the health of humanity. Industrial agriculture cannot possibly provide *long-run* global food security.

Contrary to popular belief, the failure of industrial agriculture to provide food security is readily apparent in the United States. In fact, a larger percentage of Americans are food insecure today than during the 1960s, prior to the final phases of agricultural industrialization.[6] More than 20% of American children today live in food insecure homes. Food security means that everyone must have enough wholesome and nutritious food to support healthy, active lifestyles. Food insecurity takes on a different form in nations with industrial food economics. The food insecure people in these nations can often get enough food to satisfy their need for calories or energy but do not get enough nutritious food to meet their nutritional needs for healthy, active lifestyles. Diet related illnesses are rampant in America, including obesity and related diseases such as diabetes, hypertension, heart failure, and various types of cancers. These illnesses are prevalent in lower-income, food-insecure homes.

Obesity related illnesses alone are projected to claim about one-in-five dollars spent for health care in America by 2020, erasing virtually all of the gains made in improving public health over the past several decades.[7] A growing body of scientific evidence links the industrialization of agriculture to foods that are rich in calories and poor in essential nutrients, which have helped fuel the epidemic of obesity and other diet-related illnesses in America.[8] The rising costs of diet-related health care have paralleled the industrialization of agriculture. Industrial agriculture in America has produced an abundance of cheap food, but it has failed to provide food security.

Agricultural industrialization has also failed to increase food security in the so-called developing nations. A larger percentage of people in the world are hungry today than were hungry prior to the Green Revolution. The development experts attribute the persistent increases in global hunger to increases in population made possible by increased food production. However, many of those living in developing nations often have a very different view. In the words of Stacia and Kristof Nordin who have worked for years with farmers in Malawi, Africa:

> Another drawback to the new [Green Revolution] varieties of crops is their reliance on chemical fertilizers and pesticides to ensure the success of a harvest. This process continually denies the return of organic matter to the nature cycle, the very essence of soil structure. As this depletion of organic matter has taken its

toll, farmers have resorted to purchasing and applying greater quantities of chemicals to make up the difference. When these farmers, especially in developing countries, have been faced with these issues many have found themselves caught in a cycle of dependency that has actually left them worse off than before the Green Revolution took hold. People are finding that they are forced to sell off larger amounts of their yields in order to cover the cost of these growing expenditures. The selling of their crops has deprived many families of annual food reserves, nutritional requirements, and increased standards of living. As this cycle of dependency widens, the alternatives for creating healthy lifestyles seem to be narrowing.[9]

Vandava Shiva, a globally-prominent and highly-respected ecologist and Indian food activist summarizes the failure as follows:

> The Green Revolution has been a failure. It has led to reduced genetic diversity, increased vulnerability to pests, soil erosion, water shortages, reduced soil fertility, micronutrient deficiencies, soil contamination, reduced availability of nutritious food crops for the local population, the displacement of vast numbers of small farmers from their land, rural impoverishment and increased tensions and conflicts. The beneficiaries have been the agrochemical industry, large petrochemical companies, manufacturers of agricultural machinery, dam builders and large landowners.[10]

Industrial agriculture inevitably increases hunger in developing countries because [it] displaces subsistence farming families, who are meeting at least most of their basic food needs, and fails to provide them with economic opportunities to purchase foods they are no longer able to produce for themselves. Subsistence farmers typically rely on selling some amount of surplus production to meet specific needs that they cannot meet from their farming operations. Such needs may include clothing, medical care, school fees, and transportation. Industrial agriculture invariably is introduced on larger, specialized farms, often with generous government subsidies, because it is incompatible with small, diversified, family farms. The increase in production on these larger farms depresses market prices for the agricultural commodities that subsistence farmers must sell to meet their financial needs, thus often depriving them of their ability to continue farming. This frees up farmland for industrial farms but forces subsistence farmers into the cities in search of employment.

Urban employment for displaced farmers often is not available or doesn't pay enough to meet the food needs of their families. Thus, families that were once reasonably well-fed on subsistence farms are now among the hungry. The experts assume the increased calorie production on industrial farms must have reduced hunger. However, the loss in production on subsistence farms was never accurately counted and thus represents an unknown and often ignored offsetting loss in calorie production due to industrialization. The fact that previous food-importing countries become food exporters simply means the new industrial producers are exporting their products to more profitable markets, rather than selling to poor, hungry people at home. The potential reduction in food prices for those living in the cities is often too small to make any real difference in hunger even in the cities. In addition, reductions in production costs may be offset by increased profits of food processors and distributors and the nutritional quality of food may be diminished, as it has been in the United States. Even in cases where it may appear that industrial agriculture has succeeded, it eventually is destined to fail.

The unsustainability of industrial agriculture is inherent in the industrial model or paradigm of production. Industrialization is motivated by economic efficiency. Efficiency is determined by economic value relative to economic costs. Economic values and costs are determined by scarcity, meaning the quantity of something that is available relative to the quantity that people are willing and able to buy. The industrial revolution advanced most rapidly in those nations and situations where there was a scarcity of labor and management ability relative to land and capital. Industrialization was a new model of organization that allowed production to be increased by relying more on specialized tools, machinery, and equipment and relying less on labor and management. The new technologies eventually included fertilizers and pesticides as well as fossil fuels and machinery and equipment for industrial farming. Financial capital provided the means of acquiring and using industrial technologies. Capital and technology were substituted for labor and management for people.

The basic strategies of industrialization are specialization, standardization, and consolidation of control. By specializing in producing specific crops of livestock or phases of crop and livestock production, the specific tasks could be carried out more efficiently, meaning by employing fewer farmers. Specialization required standardization, simplification, and routinization of each task and each phase of production so they could be coordinated to complete the entire production process. Standardization allowed control or management of the production process to be consolidated into few larger farming operations, meaning fewer farm managers. This is the process by which industrialization achieves economies of scale, allowing fewer farmers on larger farms to produce more food.

In addition, standardization and simplification inevitably result in the deskilling of the agricultural workforce. Thoughtful, caring farmers are replaced with farm workers who are trained to follow instructions and eventually become capable of performing only simple tasks. The economic costs of labor and management are reduced, but fewer people are employed and those who are employed contribute less to the economy. The economic benefits accrue largely to the few who manage large agricultural operations, the corporate managers who employ or contract with them, and to the stockholders in the large corporations that ultimately dominate or control industrial food systems.

Industrial agriculture cannot provide global food security. But is there an alternative? Can an agriculture that is sustainable over the long run meet the growing food needs of global society over the next fifty years? If we can't feed the world with large, specialized, mechanized farms, can we provide global food security with small, diversified, organic farms? Contrary to what is commonly believed, that question has been asked and answered. No one can foretell the future with certainty, but small, diversified, organic family farms are humanity's best hope for global food security.

[…]

References

1. David and Marcia Pimentel, *Food, Energy, and Society* (Niwot, CO: University Press of Colorado), 1996.

2. Judith S. Soule and John K. Piper, *Farming in Nature's Image, An Ecological Approach to Agriculture* (Washingtion, DC: Island Press, 1992).

3. Fred Kirschenmann, Cultivating an Ecological Conscience (Berkeley, CA: Counterpoint, 2010).

4. Dana Cordell, Jan-Olof Drangert, and Stuart White, (May 2009). "The Story of Phosphorus: Global Food Security and Food for Thought," *Global Environmental Change* (Elsevier) 19 (2): 292-305. doi:10.1016/j.gloenvcha.2008.10.009. Also, Natasha Gilbert, (8 October 2009). "The Disappearing Nutrient," *Nature* 461: 716-718. doi:10.1038/461716a.

5. Wikipedia, "Greenhouse Gas," http://en.wikipedia.org/wiki/Greenhouse_gas and "Climate Change and Agriculture," http://en.wikipedia.org/wiki/Climate_change _and_agriculture.

6. USDA, Household Food Security in the US, ERS: Economic Research Report No. 125, Sept. 2011. http://www.ers.usda.gov/Publications/ERR125/ERR125.pdf.

7. "Cost of Treatment for Obesity-Related Medical Problems Growing Dramatically," *Rand Corporation.* http://www.rand.org/news/press.04/03.09.html.

8. For Example: Donald Davis, Melvin Epp, and Hugh Riordan, 2004, "Changes in USDA Food Composition Data for 43 Garden Crops, 1950 to 1999," *Journal of American College of Nutrition*, 23:669-682. Bob Smith, 1993, "Organic Foods vs. Supermarket Foods: Element Levels," *Journal of Applied Nutrition*, 45:35-39. WM Jarrell and RB Beverly, 1981, "The Dilution Effect in Plant Nutrient Studies," *Advances in Agronomy*, 34:197-224.

9. Stacia and Kristof Nordin, "Green Revolution Fails," *Never Ending Food*, a Permaculture Nutrition Training Manual available from the authors (2000). http://www.neverendingfood.org/articles/how-the-green-revolution-has-failed-to-feed -us/.

10. Vandana Shiv, "The Green Revolution in the Punjab," *The Ecologist*, Vol. 21, No. 2, March-April 1991. http://livingheritage.org/green-revolution.htm.

Agribusiness's Reliance on Monocultures Contributes to Hunger

Kumi Naidoo

Kumi Naidoo is the current Secretary-General of Amnesty International. He is active in environmental and human rights campaigns, and has worked with Greenpeace, Civicus, the Global Call to Action Against Poverty, and the Helping Hands Youth Organisation.

On today's United Nations biodiversity day, we are being asked to focus on small islands and their unique ecology and fragility in times of globally pervasive threats such as climate change.

But, the whole planet is a small island in the vast sea of space, capable of producing food for all as a consequence of rich biodiversity. That diversity is under threat, our actions can strengthen it or weaken it. Our agriculture systems can help mitigate climate change and feed us, or they can accelerate the change and contribute to hunger.

The food system we choose has a direct impact on which type of world we will have. It's the difference between a field that hums and is robust with life, or one which is dusty, dry and dead. It's the difference between a place where ecological farming has been used or where a cocktail of industrial chemicals has soaked into the soil where the same crop is grown, decade after decade.

Our current food and farming system is creating more and more of these dry, dead ends. It is agriculture characterised by three things: the industrial-sized growing of a single plant, or "monoculture," genetically engineered crops, and repeated toxic chemical infusions of pesticides and the application of synthetic fertilisers. All of these harm people and the farming ecosystems they depend on.

"The Food System We Choose Affects Biodiversity: Do We Want Monocultures?" by Kumi Naidoo, Guardian News and Media Limited, May 22, 2014. Reprinted by permission.

Just one example of the consequences of the current flawed agricultural system is the current catastrophic bee decline. Bees are being decimated in Europe and North America by the intensive use of chemical pesticides. In recent winters bee mortality in Europe has averaged at about 20%. A third of the food that we eat every day depends on bees and other insect pollinators.

This dead-end road sees large multinational corporations persuading farmers to buy genetically engineered (GE) seeds based on the premise that they will increase yields, despite studies suggesting otherwise. Instead, they only increase farmers' indebtedness by failing to deliver the promised return on investment—turning them into slaves to a pesticide treadmill as superweeds develop. This is the ugly story behind the majority of the food we consume.

This cycle increases our dependency on fossil fuels and contributes to climate change, as the Intergovernmental Panel on Climate Change (IPCC) study recently reported. In fact, climate change affects this broken food system. Among other impacts, climate shocks cause food prices to rise, with deadly consequences in developing countries.

Climate change is estimated to have increased the amount spent on food worldwide by $50bn a year. Climate change is also making food less nutritious according to a study published in *Nature*, with important staple crops such as wheat and maize containing fewer essential nutrients like zinc and iron. Projections show that up to 21% more children globally will be at risk of hunger by 2050.

Industrial agriculture does not rely on diversification but on the standardisation and homogenisation of biological processes, technologies and products. It promotes off-the-shelf, one-size-fits-all solutions to food and farming around the world and in so doing undermines local and natural diversity, which are essential for resilience to climate change.

Ecological farming increases resilience to climate shocks. It is based on the diversity of nature to produce healthy food for all: diversity of seeds and plants; diversity of many different crops grown in the same field; diversity of insects that pollinate (like bees) or eliminate pests; and diversity of farming systems that mix crops with livestock.

Scientists from Wageningen University in the Netherlands, for example, recently found that certain beans greatly improve poor soils, increase productivity of maize when grown together and respond well to drought. They can be used for food, animal feed, and soil fertility. Researchers found that growing maize and beans at the same time increased farmers' income by 67% without the use of any chemical fertilisers.

Ecological farming also relies on the innovations of farmers that enable adaptation to local conditions. It's the redeployment of traditional knowledge to counteract the impacts of climate change. In north-east Thailand, jasmine rice farmers have been adapting to increased drought by finding creative ways to use water resources—stock ponds for storage and simple wind-powered pumps made with locally available materials—which have been shown to increase yields and provide a safety net when drought strikes.

Ecological farming effectively contributes to climate change mitigation. Industrial farming is a massive greenhouse gas (GHG) emitter. Agriculture, in fact, accounts for between 17% and 32% of all the emissions caused by humans, according to research for Greenpeace. Stopping chemical nitrogen fertiliser overuse and shifting to organic fertilisers (to increase soil fertility), improving water management in paddy rice production, and increasing agro-biodiversity through agroforestry are just a few examples of how ecological farming practices and diversity could directly contribute to GHG reduction and help agriculture reduce the effects of climate change.

Agriculture is now at a crossroads: we can pursue the dystopian dead-end road of industrial chemical-intensive farming or choose diverse and resilient ecological farming.

Governments, donors, philanthropists and the private sector must start shifting funds towards research to generate new knowledge on biodiversity-rich ecological farming and services to disseminate diversified practices that are locally relevant. We must reject the dead-end trap of industrial agriculture and choose instead a food system that celebrates biodiversity and is healthy for people and the planet.

Genetically Modified Organisms (GMOs) Provide the Key to Global Food Security

Ramez Naam

Ramez Naam is the founder of Apex Nano-Technologies, a company focused on accelerating molecular design through software tools. He is also the author of several books, including The Infinite Resource: The Power of Ideas on a Finite Planet *(2013).*

The folks at Grist have kindly allowed me to pen a guest post here with a few thoughts on Nathanael Johnson's excellent series on genetically modified foods and in particular his most recent piece on what he learned from 6 months investigating the GMO debate: that none of it really matters.

This most recent piece nails several key points that often go completely missed. When we get down to the specifics, we find that today's GMOs are neither planetary panacea nor unbridled poison. The passionate, emotion-filled debate is more about the lenses through which we see the world as it is about genetically modified foods themselves. The GMO debate is often an emphatic and barely-disguised metaphor for our larger debate about whether technology is destroying the world or saving it, whether we should try to control nature or live within it.

That's not to say the debate, when it touches on GMOs themselves, is balanced. The scientific consensus is that GMOs are as safe to eat as any other food, that they reduce soil-damaging tillage, reduce carbon emissions, reduce insecticide use, and reduce the use of the most toxic herbicides in favor of far milder ones. GMOs have limitations, and some of their benefits are threatened by the rise of pesticide resistance. Even so, on balance, GMOs are safe and produce real benefits. As I wrote at *Discover* magazine last year, GMOs achieve many of the goals of organic agriculture.

(To balance that out, let me state that I also wrote there that GMO supporters should embrace sensible GMO labeling.)

But Johnson is also right that, in the US, the stakes are not at present world-changing. US farmers could likely get by without GMOs. We might see upticks in toxic pesticide use and river runoffs, in soil-harming tillage, and in carbon emissions, but none of those would prove catastrophic. There might be a very slight reduction in crop yield, but not by much, and not for long. The vast majority of us would never notice.

In that context, I agree that the current debate is more about abstractions, metaphors, and worldviews than it is about the realities on the ground.

Even so, I think there are two important reasons we *should* care about GMOs, and view them, certainly not as panaceas, but as imperfect but important tools that can improve the lives of millions of people *right now* and possibly have an impact on *billions* of lives and millions of square miles of nature in the decades to come.

Why We Should Care—The Long Term

The Food and Agriculture Organization of the UN estimates that we need to grow 70 percent more food by 2050. Either we do this on the same land we have today, or we chop down forest to create farms and pastures to meet that demand, something no one wants to do.

Jon Foley at the Institute on the Environment points out, quite rightly, that it's meat consumption, not population, that's driving global food demand. So we could, instead, reduce meat consumption. That's a noble goal. Unfortunately, meat consumption has roughly quadrupled in the last 50 years, primarily driven by increasing wealth in the developing world, with no sign of stopping. I welcome any practical plan to reduce meat consumption worldwide, but until then, we have to find a way to keep boosting food production.

Another way to feed the world is to close the "yield gap" between farms in the rich and poor worlds. Farmers in the US grow twice as much food per acre as the world overall, largely because they can afford farm equipment, fuel, fertilizer, and pesticides that many farmers in the developing world can't. Some of this gap, undoubtedly, will be closed as poverty drops around the world. But it's unrealistic to assume that all of it will.

What are we to do? On the horizon are some GMOs in development that could provide a dramatic boost here.

1. **Better photosynthesis.** Corn and sugarcane grow nearly twice as much food per acre as the crops humans eat most: rice and wheat. Why? Corn and sugarcane have a better way of doing photosynthesis—of turning light, plus water, plus CO_2 into carbohydrates. This newer system is called C4 photosynthesis. Researchers around the world—funded by nonprofits like the Gates Foundation—are working on creating C4 Rice and C4 Wheat. Those crops could grow 50 percent more food per acre.

2. **Self-fertilizing crops.** Fertilizer boosts plant growth by adding nitrogen, and access to fertilizer is one reason rich nation farms grow so much more food per acre than their developing world counterparts. But fertilizer runoff is also responsible for the Gulf dead zone and similar zones around the world. Some crops, though, can fertilize themselves by pulling nitrogen from the air. Legumes, like soy, peas, and clover do this. Another nonprofit funded GMO research area is to transfer this ability to cereal crops, creating self-fertilizing wheat, corn, and rice. That would have two advantages: It would boost yields for poor farmers who can't afford additional fertilizer; and it would cut down on nitrogen runoff that creates these ocean dead zones.

These are just two projects among many, along with creating more drought-resistant crops, more salt-resistant crops, and crops that have higher levels of vitamins and minerals that people need.

Now, let me be very clear. Most of these are research projects. They're not in the here and now. They're not going to arrive this year, and probably not in the next 10 years. And we do continue to make great progress in improving crops through conventional breeding. But we're unlikely to ever get to, say, C4 rice or C4 wheat through conventional breeding.

The bigger point here isn't that we absolutely need GMOs to feed the future world. If we banned all future GMO development and planting, we'd most likely muddle through in some way. Humanity is good at innovating, particularly when our back is to the wall. But we'd be fighting this battle to keep increasing food output with one arm tied behind our back. We might make *less* progress in boosting yields, without GMOs, meaning food prices would be higher, hunger would be higher, or we'd have more pressure to chop down forests to grow food.

Or maybe we'd be just fine. But given the size of the challenge, and the absence of any credible evidence of harm from GMOs, robbing ourselves of this part of our toolkit strikes me as foolish.

Why We Should Care—The Here and Now

The future's easy to discount. So let's come back to the present, and in particular, the present reality for the 6 billion people who live outside of the rich world.

Until recently, the majority of the acres of GM farmland in the world have been in rich nations. Today, the US ranks first, followed by Brazil and Argentina (what we'd call middle income nations), and then Canada (another rich nation). That means that when we look at how GM crops perform, we tend to focus on how they do in countries where farmers have access to farm equipment, fertilizer, pesticides, irrigation, and so on. And in those countries we see a real but modest benefit.

In the developing world, it's markedly different.

India allows only one genetically modified crop: GM cotton with the Bt trait, which makes the cotton naturally resistant to insects and reduces the need to spray insecticides. In the US, there's a broad consensus that Bt corn has reduced insecticide spraying (which is good) but less evidence that it's increased how much food is actually produced per acre, at least to a significant degree. In India, where quite a large number of farmers can't readily afford pesticides, and where they lack farm equipment, meaning that pesticides must be applied by hand, the situation is dramatically different.

For the decade between 1991 and 2001, cotton yields in India were flat, at around 300 kilograms per hectare (a hectare is about 2.5 acres). In 2002, Bt cotton was introduced into the country. Farmers adopted it quickly, and yields of cotton soared by *two thirds* in just a few years to more than 500 kilograms per hectare.

Between 1975 and 2009, researchers found that Bt cotton produced 19 percent of India's yield growth, despite the fact that it was only on the market for 8 of those 24 years. The simpler view is that Bt cotton, in India, lifts yields by somewhere between 50 percent and 70 percent.

Why does this matter? There are 7 million cotton farmers in India. Several peer reviewed studies have found that, because Bt cotton increases the amount of crop they have to sell, it raises their farm profits by as much as 50 percent, helps lift them out of poverty and reduces their risk of falling into hunger. By reducing the amount of insecticide used (which, in India, is mostly sprayed by hand) Bt cotton has also massively reduced insecticide poisoning to farm workers there—to the tune of 2.4 *million* cases per year.

You may perhaps be wondering: Don't GMOs lead to more farmer suicides in India? And while farmer suicides in India are real, and each one is a tragedy, the link is false. Farmer suicides have been going on long before GMOs, and, if anything, the farmer suicide rate has slightly dropped since the introduction of GM seeds.

In China we've seen similar impacts of Bt cotton, with multiple studies showing that Bt cotton increased yields, boosted the incomes of 4 million smallholder farmers, and reduced pesticide poisoning among them.

All of this is to say that GM crops have more impact in poor countries than rich ones. Where other types of inputs, like fertilizers, farm equipment, and pesticides are harder to afford, GM crops have more to offer. That can help increase food, reduce pressure on deforestation, and lift farmers out of poverty.

But the world's poorest countries, and in particular India and the bulk of sub-Saharan Africa, don't allow any GM *food crops* to be grown. India came close to approval for a Bt eggplant (or Bt brinjal). Studies showed that it was safe, that it could cut pesticide use by half, and that it could nearly double yields by reducing losses to insects. But, while India's regulators approved the planting and sale, activists cried out, prompting the government to place an indefinite moratorium on it. Similar things have happened elsewhere. The same Bt eggplant was supported by regulators in the Philippines who looked at the data, but then blocked by the court on grounds that reflected not specific concerns, but general, metaphorical, and emotional arguments that Nathanael Johnson describes as dominating the debate.

That's a pity. Because if Bt food crops could produce similar size gains in the developing world, that would be a tremendous benefit. Insect losses are a tremendously larger challenge in India and Africa than in the US. Boosting the amount of food that a farm produces by half or more means less hunger, more income for farmers (still the majority of the population in the world's poorest countries), and more ability of people to pull themselves out of poverty.

The same arguments that kept Bt eggplant out of the Philippines have also been used, often by western groups, to keep GM crops out of virtually all of Africa, as documented by Robert Paarlberg in his powerful (and to some, infuriating) book *Starved For Science*.

I have absolutely no doubt that the opponents of genetically modified foods, and particularly those campaigning against their planting in the developing world, are doing this with the best of intentions. They fully believe that they're protecting people in Africa, India, the Philippines, and elsewhere against poisons, against corporate control of their food, or against destruction of their environment. Yet I wish more of them would read Nathanael Johnson's carefully thought-out series here and in particular his argument that most of the debate is highly inflamed.

Most of the perceived ills of genetically modified foods are either illusory or far smaller than believed. And what the data suggests is that the benefits, while modest in the rich world today, might be quite substantial in the future, and are already much larger in the parts of the world where the battle over GMO approval is most actively raging.

GMOs are neither poison nor panacea. What they are is a toolkit, a varied one, with real benefits to the environment and millions of people today; with the real potential to have a larger positive impact *immediately* if they're allowed to; and with the possibility of a dramatically larger benefit down the road as the science behind them improves.

Industrial Agriculture Can Be Part of the Fight Against Hunger in Developing Countries

Cristian Torres-León, Nathiely Ramírez-Guzman, Liliana Londoño-Hernandez, Gloria A. Martinez-Medina, Rene Díaz-Herrera, Víctor Navarro-Macias, Olga B. Alvarez-Pérez, Brian Picazo, Maria Villarreal-Vázquez, Juan Ascacio-Valdes, and Cristóbal N. Aguilar

The authors are members of the Group of Bioprocesses and Bioproducts in the School of Chemistry's Food Research Department at Universidad Autónoma de Coahuila in Saltillo, Mexico.

Agricultural production and agro-industrial processing generate a high amount of byproducts and waste. Fruit byproducts such as bagasse, peels, trimmings, stems, shells, bran, and seeds account for more than 50% of fresh fruit and have at times a nutritional or functional content higher than the final product. Fruit and food waste is also generated by damage during transportation, storage, and processing. The growing popularity of fruit juices, nectars, frozen and minimally processed products has also increased the production of byproducts and wastes in recent years.

Byproducts and waste generation are having an impact on environmental, economic, and social sectors. To the environment, these contribute to Green House Gas (GHG) emissions. Many of these biomaterials are not utilized and end up in municipal landfills where they create serious environmental problems due to microbial decomposition and leachate production. In some cases,

"Food Waste and Byproducts: An Opportunity to Minimize Malnutrition and Hunger in Developing Countries," by Cristian Torres-León, Nathiely Ramírez-Guzman, Liliana Londoño-Hernandez, Gloria A. Martinez-Medina, Rene Díaz-Herrera, Víctor Navarro-Macias, Olga B. Alvarez-Pérez, Brian Picazo, Maria Villarreal-Vázquez, Juan Ascacio-Valdes, and Cristóbal N. Aguilar, *Frontiers in Sustainable Food Systems*, September 4, 2018. https://www.frontiersin.org/articles/10.3389/fsufs.2018.00052/full. Licensed under CC BY 4.0 International.

the byproducts are burned to remove fungi and parasites. From the economic point of view, the adverse impact is due to the costs related to the handling of solid waste in landfills. Moreover, the management of large amounts of different degradable materials poses a challenge.

Social impacts may be attributed to an ethical and moral dimension within the general concept of global food security since 805 million people across the globe suffer from hunger (FAO, 2014). To manage the nutritional problems of today's society, we require more composite nutritional sources. Food wastes and byproducts are of paramount importance here due to the presence of sufficient quantities of proteins, lipids, starch, micronutrients, bioactive compounds, and dietary fibers. Protein deficiency and associated malnutrition is one of the serious problems in most of the developing countries. Food fortification serves as a crucial strategy to fight malnutrition and important initiatives have been undertaken to utilize residues and byproducts in Europe and USA. Poorer nations where the problems of malnutrition and hunger exists at a higher level, there is a greater potential of exploitation of these biomaterials as they generate large quantities of byproducts. The main raw materials used in the industries in such countries are fruits, vegetables, dairy products and fish. Tropical and subtropical fruits like mango, pineapple, banana, grape, and citrus are important fruits used in processing in poor countries.

The utilization of residues and byproducts generated in the poor regions of the world for the formulation of novel foods will directly benefit the local communities. In Nigeria, for example, the use of mango byproducts has been suggested as the main ingredient in the diet of infants and adults since it increases the content of protein and antioxidants. A strategy to reduce malnutrition and hunger in developing countries is the use of food wastes and byproducts as a source of food additives or as a raw material for the feeding of animals for human consumption. Value-added product generation can benefit infrastructure development, transportation, food processing, and packaging industries. This contributes to the reduction in waste accumulation and results in significant financial benefits. Tropical fruits, dairy, and fish are an important commercial food and crop enterprise, which plays an important role in the socio-economic development of rural and urban populations in countries in Africa, Asia, and America. For example in Kenya, the production chain of mango and mango derived products contributes significantly to the agricultural Gross Domestic Product (GDP) and foreign exchange earnings. Therefore, the diversification of the chain with the valorization of byproducts will generate income and create employment opportunities for residents which will directly benefit poor communities. To achieve the Millennium Development Goals related to hunger and malnutrition, we need to address poverty.

The depletion of renewable resources, reduction in land for cultivation, continuous growth of the world population and the over accumulation of waste are factors that justify the utilization of waste and byproducts in the food sector. Despite the wide potential of byproducts as materials for the formulation of foods, some may present low digestibility absorption due to the presence of anti-nutritional compounds such as tannins, cyanogenic glycosides, oxalates, and trypsin inhibitory substances (Arogba, 1997). This highlights the need to develop novel processes to reduce these nutritional factors from food wastes.

The experience of Europe shows that although there is legislation aimed at the use of waste in the production of biofuels, many of the small merchants do not fulfill with the norms and dispose of the wastes in the environment. Additionally, the Environmental Protection Agency (EPA, 2017) had set a priority to use the surplus to feed the hungry people first, then animals, and finally industrial uses, composting and incineration. The process of incineration of waste attracted attention because the combustion process releases highly toxic pollutants.

Proper use of food waste and byproducts as raw materials or food additives, could generate economic gains for the industry, contribute to reducing nutritional problems, would produce beneficial health effects and would reduce the environmental implications that generate mismanagement of waste. Presently, the industries are interested in innovations so as to obtain zero waste, where the waste generated is used as raw material for new products and applications. These actions can directly impact the Millennium Development Goals, the upcoming Sustainable Development Goals, the Post 2015 Agenda and the Zero Hunger Challenge. In this context, the main goal of this review article is to present the potential of food waste and byproducts as a sustainable alternative to reduce malnutrition and hunger in developing countries. The following examples have been chosen as being a contrasting set of materials for which much information is available and for which clear improvements and opportunities are envisaged.

[…]

Research and Innovation

Use of Food Wastes and Byproducts as Food Ingredients

The food demand all over the world is increasing and there is a need to develop new foods or make better some of the known. Food development applying food wastes or byproducts from different agro-industries is a great alternative to make using some secondary food products. Many or almost all these products are always discarded, and they can be improved to make some foods like cookies or cereal bars as an example. Not all agro-industrial wastes can be used as an ingredient in a newly developed food and it can't be any kind of food, usually the foods developed using agro-industrial wastes are the ones made with flours.

There are some wastes which are used to fortify some foods. For example, tortilla added with defatted soybean meal increase the protein content, soy flour has been added to spaghetti too and it has increased the protein and amino acid content. King palm flour was used in the production of cookies and gluten-free cookies for obtaining a higher yield of dietary fiber and some minerals like calcium, magnesium or potassium (Vieira et al., 2008; De Simas et al., 2009).

Paiva et al. (2012), used the core of the pineapple and merged it with another ingredient like soybean extracts and broken rice to produce a new cereal bar with high protein, dietary fiber and mineral content and low caloric value. Díaz Vela et al. (2015), applied pineapple peel flour to improve the physicochemical properties of cooked sausages and they got a great performance but compared with cactus pear peel flour, pineapple peel flour was not found better. It retains water in sausages and decreases oxidative rancidity. As presented in section Mango, mango rind is also a good source of dietary fiber; mango peel flour can be added in the formulation of pasta (macaroni), bakery products (bread, cakes, and cookies), dairy products (cheese, yogurt, and ice cream) and extruded foods. All these food products have a great relevance in the world food market.

Jabuticaba peel has been used in Brazil to develop cookies and cereal bars. Cardoso Zago et al. (2015), used jabuticaba peel to develop cookies without losing any sensorial properties of the traditional cookies. Appelt et al. (2015), combined jabuticaba peel with *Okara* instead of traditional flours and they created a new cereal bar with a high protein content and the sensorial characteristics have a great acceptability. Dischsen et al. (2013), reported that they can use cassava waste to develop a breakfast cereal in combination with corn grits as the main ingredients in preparation. The resultant product had a higher fiber content and a crispy texture compared to the cereal made only with corn grits.

Ricce et al. (2013), used powders of asparagus and almond sugar powders, artichoke bracts, and wheat bran in different combinations and the quality characteristics of the products were evaluated. The sensorial acceptance of the bread, along with these materials were very good.

The extraction of different compounds from the accumulating food wastes and byproducts create new options to utilize these extracts into food industry to make better foods. Some of the wastes can give better nutritional characteristics to the existing food including higher antioxidant property, higher protein or fiber content and high concentrations of minerals very essentials to the human health. Sun-Waterhouse et al. (2013), evaluated three different apple wastes. They reported that the three wastes from the three different apples had a considerable polypeptide concentration. The three different parts evaluated from the apples can be used in development of novel food products. There is a great opportunity for all food wastes and byproducts to be utilized for the production of diverse types of food with better nutritional characteristics. Food residues/wastes contain several compounds which are metabolized better in the human system than others. Proper utilization of these biomaterials can benefit human health, can bring advancements to the food industry and can solve many environmental problems created due to the discharge of these wastes.

Technological Perspective

Due to the nutritional, nutraceutical, and functional properties of the food waste, it can be argued that this is a raw material with significant potential and numerous applications in food formulations, mainly in the developing countries where this waste is produced. Biomolecules like proteins, lipids, starch, vitamins, minerals, fibers, and antioxidants, present in the food wastes and byproducts can be separated individually from the biological matrix (using extraction techniques physical or chemical) or used directly as a food to make the most of the nutritional and functional components contained in them. However, microbiological risks should always be avoided, so that the unitary drying operation is a fundamental step to guarantee the microbiological and physicochemical stability of biomaterials. Therefore, new government actions must be implemented to install infrastructure and technology that allows taking advantage of waste and byproducts in its places of production and storage. The new developments in infrastructure should also contemplate the possibility of reduction of ANF. In this respect, fermentation process is an effective method to eliminate ANF and fortify biomaterials.

With the appropriate preservation technology, food wastes and byproducts rich in dietary fiber can be used as food powders. The powder can be directly used in drinks, taking advantage of its good solubility. These biomaterials can also be used in the manufacture of bakery products in developing countries where tropical fruit, buttermilk, and fish waste are mainly grown and processed. New research on the development of novel products based on byproducts is very much required. Technological innovation can contribute to the promotion of new business alternatives, which will contribute to the increase in the number of beneficial foods to reduce hunger and generate more employment, which directly benefits local communities.

In the evaluation of food waste as a source of food additives legal aspects should be considered, for evaluating food safety in potential consumers. The creation of a new product for marketing purposes must have an authorization from the state entity delegated to that function. The qualification of a certain substance as food has great implications since it means that generic and specific food legislation must be applied. Finally, food products must comply with all the quality and safety requirements of the food regulations of the respective countries.

Conclusions

The development of sustainable solutions for the management of byproducts and food waste is one of the main challenges of our society. These solutions must be able to take full advantage of the biological potential of biomaterials and achieve economic, social and environmental benefits. With the nutritional problems facing society today (hunger indicators and the growing world population), the use of food waste for human food should be a priority. Wastes and byproducts produced in developing countries have a powerful nutritional and functional use in their formulation and a powerful tool in minimizing of hunger. In addition, the added value generated by the diversification of the productive chains can create job opportunities for the residents generating an additional social benefit.

CHAPTER 2

Does the Industrial Food Complex Encourage Obesity?

Obesity in America Is an Epidemic

Berkeley Wellness

Berkeley Wellness, in collaboration with the University of California Berkeley School of Public Health, provides resources and information on evidence-based wellness.

Body weight is an essential part of a person's self-image, and when pounds accumulate, so often does distress. Our culture is, to put it mildly, preoccupied with weight. Large weight gain is almost always noticed, if not discussed, and can lead to stigmatization and even discrimination.

And yet, surveys show that almost half of people who are overweight or even obese don't realize it, and most parents of obese children describe their kids as being "about the right weight."

Obesity is one of the biggest health risks we face. It increases the risk of many chronic disorders, notably heart and liver disease, hypertension, type 2 diabetes, some types of cancer, gallstones, sleep apnea, osteoarthritis, reflux disease, and respiratory problems—and it can seriously undermine quality of life.

The adverse health effects of obesity have blunted some of the gains in longevity resulting from medical advances and declining smoking rates. It's estimated that obesity is associated with anywhere from 10 to 25 percent of all deaths and shortens life expectancy by four to seven years.

Obesity rates in the US have been rising for a century and have more than doubled in just the past 35 years, affecting every ethnic, demographic, and age group. More than one-third of American adults (80 million) are now obese—that is, very overweight—and another third are slightly or moderately overweight, according to government statistics. Even worse, the rate of severe obesity (usually more than 100 pounds overweight) has more than tripled during this period. What's more, 17 percent of young Americans (ages 2 to 19) are now obese, and as many are overweight. These statistics are based on the body mass index (BMI), a formula that relates weight to height.

Obesity rates have also been climbing in Canada and other countries, though few come close to or exceed our rate (the most obese: Kuwait and Saudi Arabia).

In light of these trends, in 2013 the American Medical Association started classifying obesity as a disease, a decision that still generates debate. Also that year, the American Heart Association, the American College of Cardiology, and the Obesity Society announced in joint guidelines that obesity should be treated as a chronic disease.

Why Have We Been Gaining So Much Weight?

On the most basic level, people gain weight when there's an energy imbalance—they consume more calories than they burn. But it's overly simplistic to blame the obesity epidemic solely on people eating too much because of lack of willpower and on sedentary lifestyles. If there ever was a multifactorial condition, obesity is it—a complex of interacting genetic, metabolic, behavioral, hormonal, psychological, cultural, environmental, and socioeconomic factors, some of which are easier to alter than others.

Here's a Summary of Key Factors Involved in the Obesity Epidemic: Calories Galore

Since the 1970s, American men have increased their daily calorie intake by an average of 210 calories, and women by about 270 calories, according to an analysis in the *American Journal of Clinical Nutrition* in 2013. Calorie intake appears to have peaked about a decade ago, dropping slightly since then. Most of the extra calories have come from high-carbohydrate (that is, sugary or starchy) foods and beverages. Liquid calories are especially bad for weight control since they do not reduce appetite as much as solid foods.

"Toxic" Food Environment

One reason for our increased calorie intake: We are surrounded by inexpensive, energy-dense food, usually sold and served in oversized portions. It isn't simply that food companies profit by selling us more food, but also that people have gotten used to the abundance of cheap food (per ounce, if not per serving) and expect to find it everywhere. This calorie glut is made possible largely by government subsidies for wheat, soy, and especially corn—key ingredients in "junk" food and in feed for cattle and pigs. Other contributors to our higher calorie intake include increased and cheaper output from factory farming, improvements in food palatability (thanks to added sugar, fat, and sodium and manipulating texture and other food qualities), and marketing by the food industry.

As a result, Americans now spend a smaller share of their income on food than any society in history or anywhere else in the world (a good thing), yet we get more "empty" calories for it (not good), according to a paper about the economics of obesity, published in 2014 in *CA: A Cancer Journal of Clinicians*. This has fueled overconsumption of high-calorie fare such as fast food, corn-fed beef and pork, packaged snacks, ready-to-eat meals, and soft drinks.

Sugar Overload

Americans eat too much sugar, which has been a major player in the obesity epidemic. Sugars found naturally in foods such as fruit (mostly fructose) and milk (lactose) are not the problem. The culprit is the sugar liberally added to so many foods—not only candies and cookies, but also staples like pasta sauces, ketchup, canned baked beans, and breakfast cereals. On average, we consume about 90 grams (22 teaspoons) of added sugar a day—providing 350 calories—more than one-third from soft drinks.

The fructose in that added sugar may be a particular problem. Say fructose and most people think high-fructose corn syrup (HFCS)—the No. 1 sweetener, added to so many soft drinks and processed foods. HFCS is slightly more than half fructose, but plain old table sugar (sucrose) is also half fructose, while honey averages about 40 percent fructose. Research suggests that high intake of fructose can have adverse effects on blood cholesterol and triglycerides, worsen blood sugar control, promote abdominal fat gain, and pose other health risks. It may also have less effect on satiety than other sugars. In any case, regardless of how all this added sugar is metabolized, the main problem is that we're consuming too much of it.

Less Home Cooking

Longer average work hours and more two-worker households mean less time for home-cooked meals, especially those prepared from scratch, which tend to be more healthful and lower in calories than packaged or ready-to-eat foods. What's more, in the past few decades Americans have been eating more meals in restaurants. Studies have consistently found that restaurant fare (whether fast food or fine cuisine) tends to be higher in calories than home-cooked meals, largely because it's served in such oversized portions. Not surprisingly, then, research has linked frequent eating out to increased body weight.

Too Much Sit-Down Time

Americans are much less physically active, on average, than they were in the past. Major culprits include the increasingly sedentary nature of many forms of work; dramatically increased time spent sitting in cars, watching TV, and using computers; and lack of daily physical activity in most schools. Last year an analysis of US data in the *American Journal of Medicine* concluded that the number of women who reported no leisure-time physical activity jumped from 19 to 52 percent in the past two decades; in men the numbers rose from 11 to 43 percent. Burning fewer calories means storing more of them as body fat. And, in turn, obesity and its consequences discourage many people from exercising and staying active. Still, for most obese people, physical activity by itself, without reduction in calorie intake and improvement in diet, won't lead to significant and long-term weight loss.

Social Norms

What *should* your body look like? Look at most actors and fashion models and you may think people should have little or no body fat, a goal that is likely to set you up for failure. At the same time, if you're like most Americans and you glance at your friends, family, and neighbors, you may think that being overweight or even obese is normal.

In fact, your social network is a good predictor of whether you will be obese or not. It's not just that obese people hang out together, but also that thinner people who have many obese friends are much more likely to become obese themselves over the long term, according to a widely publicized study in the *New England Journal of Medicine* in 2007. It found that the risk increases by nearly 60 percent when a person has a friend who becomes obese and by about 40 percent when a sibling or spouse becomes obese. People of the same sex have a greater influence on each other's weight than those of the opposite sex.

Genetics and Upbringing

Obesity offers a good example of genes interacting with lifestyle and environment. It's clear that obesity runs in families: If you have an obese parent, there's a good chance you'll become obese too; with two obese parents, the risk is even greater. Part of this is explained by the fact that genes play a large role in aspects of weight regulation, such as metabolic rate (the rate at which we burn calories when at rest and during activity). Certain genes may also disrupt appetite control systems in the brain—for instance, by affecting the action of leptin, ghrelin, and other hormones that signal the brain about hunger and satiety.

Scientists have found more than 1,000 genes that affect metabolism and weight-related behavior. These help explain, for instance, why some people have an easier time staying thin (despite constant exposure to calorie-dense foods) while others continually struggle with weight gain, and why some people do better on a low-carb diet and others on a low-fat diet.

What you eat and how active you are matter too, of course, though genetics also influences your preferences for various foods and exercise and how your body responds metabolically.

Genetics may partly explain why one person becomes fat while another does not, but it doesn't explain the obesity epidemic, since human genetic makeup hasn't changed significantly during the past few generations. Here's where epigenetics comes into play. This involves changes in gene expression (not explained by changes in DNA itself) that can occur during a lifetime in response to outside influences and then be passed along to offspring. In terms of body weight, a mother's diet, weight, lifestyle, and environmental exposures before and during pregnancy can cause epigenetic changes that alter her child's risk of obesity and related conditions.

Parents also pass on or nurture other weight-related tendencies by example—regarding eating patterns, attitudes about exercise, and so on. In addition, your social stratum influences your health, habits, and body weight. For example, obesity is more prevalent among poorer people than among the well-to-do.

Too Little Sleep

Many studies over the past few years have linked inadequate sleep to an increased risk of obesity in a number of ways. Some have found that it can undermine weight-control efforts—thus, people on diets tend to be more successful when they get enough (but not too much) sleep. Other studies find that decreased sleep can lead to poorer eating habits, greater calorie intake, lower metabolic rate, and increased abdominal fat. One proposed mechanism is that not getting enough sleep affects appetite hormones, notably ghrelin and leptin, as well as insulin, leading to increased hunger and food intake, reduced calorie burning, and increased fat storage. But the relationship between sleep and metabolism is complex, and reduced sleep can affect people differently.

Inflammation and Insulin Resistance

Chronic inflammation in the body can be both a cause and an effect of insulin resistance and obesity—setting up a vicious cycle. For example, inflammation can contribute to the development of insulin resistance, which in turn may promote obesity. Conversely, obesity—especially abdominal obesity—worsens insulin resistance and increases chronic inflammation, partly because fat surrounding organs in the abdominal area (visceral fat) releases pro-inflammatory compounds. In effect, inflammation, obesity, and insulin resistance reinforce one another, often resulting in type 2 diabetes. What's more, many lifestyle factors that promote inflammation and insulin resistance, such as being sedentary and having an unhealthy diet, also promote obesity.

Microbes In the Gut

Recent research has linked the microbiota—the trillions of microorganisms in our colon—to many aspects of our health, including body weight. Animal studies have found that the composition of microbial populations in the colon influences energy metabolism as well as how carbohydrates and fats are digested, thus affecting the risk of obesity. These microbes, which vary from person to person, are influenced by genetic, dietary, environmental, and other factors. For instance, some research suggests that antibiotics, especially when given to children, may alter intestinal bacteria in ways that have long-term effects on body composition and weight.

Other "Obesogenic" Culprits

Researchers have been exploring many additional factors that may play roles in the obesity epidemic. These include various "obesogens"—chemicals in foods, products, and the environment that, in theory at least, increase fat accumulation. Some of these are endocrine disruptors, which mimic or interfere with the function of estrogen and other human hormones. We've discussed two of these: BPA, found in some hard plastics, the lining of cans, and certain paper receipts; and flame retardants used in furniture, carpeting, and mattresses. Observational studies have linked BPA exposure in the womb or in infancy to an increased risk of obesity later in life.

Other proposed obesogenic factors include certain diseases, such as hypothyroidism; increased chronic stress and lack of sense of control in modern life; older maternal age; wide use of medications associated with weight gain (such as some used for depression, diabetes, hypertension, epilepsy, and contraception); and the "addictive" properties of many seductively palatable processed foods.

Agribusiness's Influence and Unethical Food Marketing Drives Obesity in the United States

Mark Hyman

Mark Hyman, MD, is Medical Director at the Cleveland Clinic's Center for Functional Medicine. He focuses on using functional medicine to tackle the causes of chronic disease.

One third of our economy thrives on making people sick and fat. Big Farming grows 500 more calories per person per day than 25 years ago because they get paid to grow extra food even when it is not needed. The extra corn (sugar) and soy (fat) are turned into industrial processed food and sugar-sweetened beverages—combinations of fat, sugar and salt that are proven to be addictive. These subsidized ($288 billion) cheap, low-quality foods are heavily marketed ($30 billion) and consumed by our ever-widening population with an obesity rate approaching three out of four Americans. The more they eat, the fatter they become. The fatter they become the more they develop heart disease, diabetes, cancer and a myriad of other chronic ailments.

Today, one in 10 Americans have diabetes. By 2050 one in three Americans will have diabetes. The sicker our population, the more medications are sold for high cholesterol, diabetes, high blood pressure, depression, and many other lifestyle-driven diseases. The Toxic Triad of Big Farming, Big Food, and Big Pharma profits from creating a nation of sick and fat citizens.

This structure is built into the very fabric of our economy and culture. It could be called the medical, agricultural, food industrial complex. It is what is known as "structural violence"—the social, political, economic and environmental conditions that foster and promote the development of disease.

"Obesity in America: Are Factory Farms, Big Pharma and Big Food to Blame?" by Mark Hyman, *Huffington Post*, October 25, 2010. Reprinted by permission.

But there is a way to turn the Toxic Triad into a Health Trinity. Through innovation and creativity we can create a new economy based on products and services that make people thin and healthy instead of sick and fat. Business can do well by doing good! We just have to change the default choices and behaviors both at a policy and a grass-roots level. I learned a few things about this in Haiti from my friend Paul Farmer.

Addressing Structural Violence

When I was in Haiti in January 2010, after the earthquake, I visited Zanmi Lansante, the health center started in the 1980's by Dr. Paul Farmer. Much to the world's amazement he showed how, in one of the poorest places on the planet, he could successfully treat complex infectious diseases such as tuberculosis and AIDS. The conventional wisdom was that poor people sleeping on mud floors would not take complex regimens of medication so we should essentially leave them to die. The problem wasn't that doctors didn't know what medications to prescribe, but that poverty and social conditions such as lack of access to health care, food, shelter, jobs, clean water and sanitation prevented effective treatment.

Paul Farmer didn't accept this. Through his foundation, Partners in Health, with the help of the Clinton Foundation and the Gates Foundation, he demonstrated the flaws in conventional wisdom and has successfully treated "impossible to treat patients in impossible conditions" around the world. He did it because he addressed one simple thing: Structural violence.

To successfully treat people in Haiti, Paul Farmer did not simply focus on what medication regimens were needed to cure tuberculosis or treat AIDS. He "accompanied" patients into their lives. By using local, trained community health workers he helped patients change the conditions of their lives, find shelter, food, jobs, clean water and sanitation—all necessary "structural" changes that allowed for effective treatment. He addressed the system, not just the symptom.

We must do the same if we are serious about addressing the wave of chronic illness sweeping across the world. We must focus, not only on the individual, but the system that has created 1.7 billion overweight citizens worldwide if we are to slow and reverse the national and global epidemic of obesity, diabetes, and heart disease threatening not only our health, but the survival of our economies.

Big Food, Farming, and Pharma: How They Are Killing Us

The default condition of a human being in the 21st century is to be obese. Nearly 75 percent of Americans are overweight. This is not an accident. Specific, traceable forms of structural violence promoted by Big Food, Big Farming, Big Pharma and government polices is leading to the global spread of obesity, diabetes, heart disease and cancer.

Current food policies and subsidies encourage Big Farming to overproduce corn and soy which are then used to create sugary, fatty, factory-made, industrial food products sold as processed, fast, or junk food as I noted above. The government essentially stands in line next to you in fast food chains helping you buy cheeseburgers, fries, and cola. But in the produce isle of your supermarket you are on your own—the 2010 Farm Bill offers little support to farmers for growing fruits, vegetables, and healthy whole foods.

The resultant omnipresence of cheap, high-calorie, nutrient-poor processed foods (or "food like substances") in homes, schools, government institutions and food programs, and on every street corner creates default food choices that drive obesity. How can you eat fruits and vegetables when you can't buy them in your neighborhood convenience store or their price has increased five times as fast as sugar-sweetened beverages?

Big Food takes advantage of this glut of processed food to drive up profits through the use of mass media technologies. Other than drinking sugar-sweetened beverages, the number of hours of screen time or television watching is the single biggest factor correlating with obesity which, in turn, drives the diabetes epidemic. In addition to the metabolism-slowing, hypnotic effect of watching television, relentless food marketing focused on children is one of the major factors driving this problem. The average two year old can identify, by name, junk food brands in supermarkets, but many elementary school children can't readily differentiate between a potato and a tomato as Jaime Oliver recently demonstrated.

Big Food claims that the problem is one of personal responsibility—that processed foods can be part of a healthy diet as long as they are eaten in moderation. But the more we delve into the research on food marketing practices, the impact of food deserts where healthy foods simply can't be found, and the biologically addictive properties of these overly available cheap, high-calorie, nutrient poor junk/processed foods, the clearer it becomes that environmental factors override our normal physical and psychological mechanisms that control weight.

Food addiction is not a failing of personal responsibility, moral fiber, or will power that drives people to over consume these unhealthy foods. Industrial, processed food has been found to be addictive. We are like rats in a cage with unrestricted access to processed sugar and fat. When given a choice between cocaine and sugar, rats always choose sugar. So do we.

Poverty and food scarcity also drive poor food choices and are linked to obesity, and diabetes. The poverty rate in 2009 was 14.3 percent, the highest since 1994. As I pointed out in my article "Not Having Enough Food Causes Diabetes" there is a correlation between the poverty rate and the obesity rate. The poorest states in the nation are the fattest.

The government's approach to these issues echoes Big Food. Government interventions like industry initiatives are predicated on education and encouraging personal responsibility. The rhetoric is that regulating the food industry strips away our right to choose, and that the market should be self-regulating.

It's true that market-driven forces often do effectively control commerce. Companies can produce and sell poor-quality products, and if consumers choose to not buy them, the market regulates itself—companies begin supplying what consumers demand instead. This model works in our society unless those products affect our health, safety, or the greater social good. In this case, we expect our government to step in and take action.

Consider cars or medication. The government has mandated the production of safer, less polluting cars and protects us from harmful medication. In cases like these, government regulation is accepted. Poor diet causes many more deaths than auto accidents, yet as a society we resist government regulation over Big Food. Why?

If our normal protective biological mechanisms don't work in this toxic food environment—and they don't—it is lack of government oversight that erodes personal freedom. Big Food may make the right "noises," but it will not self-regulate just as Big Tobacco wouldn't.

Perhaps more to the point, there is an element of blaming the victim in all of this that misses the structural violence—the environmental conditions—that drive obesity and disease and lead to what is not being called an "obesogenic" environment. The main factors of which are:

1. **Industrial processed, fast, and junk food is addictive.** Processed food full of sugar, fat, and salt is neurochemically, biologically addictive in the same way cocaine, heroin, nicotine and caffeine are addictive, and it increases food and calorie consumption and obesity as a result.

2. **Big Farming's influence over the global increase in obesity.** Agricultural practices and government subsidies promote the growing of cheap corn and soy which is turned into the sugar, fat, and processed food that drives disease and fosters the spread of this cheap, calorie-dense, nutrient-poor food across the globe.

3. **Unethical, manipulative food marketing that drives eating habits.** There is very little government control over

Big Food's marketing practices which shape behavior in insidious ways, especially in children.

4. **Poverty's relationship to obesity and disease.** Poverty promotes obesity, diabetes, and chronic disease because processed food is cheap while being high in calories and low in nutrients.

5. **The destruction of the family kitchen and home cooked meals.** The family meal, and family and local food culture, has been replaced with convenience or fast foods. This has led to a generation of Americans who can't recognize any vegetable or fruit in its original form and can't cook except in a microwave.

6. **Obesity is contagious.** You are more likely to be obese if you have fat friends, than if you have fat relatives. Social norms promote weight gain.

7. **Environmental toxins.** These contribute to weight gain, obesity, and diabetes. Not only do we have to worry about what we eat, but also the burden of plastics, metals, and pollutants which have been shown to poison and slow our metabolism leading to weight gain.

Important initiatives have been created by the Obama administration within the health care bill and Michelle Obama's "Let's Move" program that mark a beginning of a shift that needs to happen in our food climate, but to really change our obesogenic environment we need to create healthier default choices for citizens. We must focus on specific actions we can take personally and politically to alter our food landscape.

[…]

If pushed, Big Farming can start growing healthy food to feed the nation and Big Food can come up with innovative solutions that satisfy consumers and supply healthful, economical, convenient, and delicious foods for our world. However, these industries will not police themselves.

Agribusiness's Oversize Food Portions Result in Obesity

Lisa R. Young and Marion Nestle

Lisa R. Young, PhD, RDN, and CDN, is a nutritionist, author, lecturer, and adjunct professor of nutrition at New York University. Marion Nestle is an author and the Paulette Goddard Professor of Nutrition, Food Studies, and Public Health at New York University.

The prevalence of overweight and obesity has increased sharply among US adults and children in recent years.[1-3] Although multiple factors can account for weight gain, the basic cause is an excess of energy intake over expenditure. If, as has been reported, activity patterns have not changed much in the past decade,[4,5] the rise in body weights must be caused by increased energy intake. Indeed, dietary intake surveys indicate a per capita increase of 200 kcal/d from 1977–1978[6] to 1994–1996,[7] and the US food supply (total food produced, less exports, plus imports) now provides 500 kcal/d per capita more than in the 1970s.[8] Regardless of how imprecise such figures may be, they appear to confirm that Americans consume more energy than they did in the past.

At issue is the cause of this increase. An obvious suggestion is food consumed outside the home, which accounted for 34% of the food budget in 1970[9] but 47% by the late 1990s.[10] Another possibility is the size of food portions. Many observations hint that out-of-home portion sizes are increasing.[11] Larger portions not only contain more energy but also encourage people to eat more,[12-14] making it more difficult to balance static levels of physical activity. Although federal dietary advice is to choose "sensible portions,"[15] these portions are not defined except by US Department of Agriculture (USDA) standards given in the food

"The Contribution of Expanding Portion Sizes to the US Obesity Epidemic," by Lisa R. Young and Marion Nestle, *American Journal of Public Health*, February 2012; 92(2): 246-249. Reprinted by permission.

guide pyramid[16] and US Food and Drug Administration (FDA) standards for food labels.[17] Both agencies base standards, in part, on information reported in dietary intake surveys,[18,19] but the standards appear to be smaller than marketplace portions. Because such discrepancies may confuse people who are attempting to follow dietary advice[20] and because little information is available on the current sizes of marketplace portions, we measured and compared food weights with those offered in the past and with USDA and FDA standards.

Methods

We sampled foods sold for immediate consumption in the most popular take-out establishments, fast-food outlets, and family-type restaurants; such places account for much of the recent increase in out-of-home food consumption, rank highest in sales, and exhibit the highest growth rates.[9,21,22] We sampled foods such as white-bread products, cakes, alcoholic beverages, steak, and sodas that represent food categories reported in national surveys as major contributors of energy to US diets and are marketed as single servings.[23,24] We obtained information about portion weights from package labels or from manufacturers. If such information was unavailable, and to confirm the accuracy of reported information, we weighed at least 2 samples of each food with a calibrated Sysco Digital Portion Scale (Model SDS-10) and recorded average weights. We compared portion weights with standard portions established by USDA for dietary guidance[16] and by FDA for food labels.[19] We obtained information about the sizes of foods offered in past years directly from manufacturers or indirectly from examination of trade publications, professional journals, marketing and advertising materials, menu collections, cookbooks, guides to fast foods, and older editions of food composition tables. Details about these methods and their validation are described elsewhere.[25]

Results

With the single exception of sliced white bread, all of the commonly available food portions we measured exceeded—sometimes greatly—USDA and FDA standard portions. The largest excess over USDA standards (700%) occurred in the cookie category, but cooked pasta, muffins, steaks, and bagels exceeded USDA standards by 480%, 333%, 224%, and 195%, respectively. Our data indicate that the sizes of current marketplace foods almost universally exceed the sizes of those offered in the past. When foods such as beer and chocolate bars were introduced, they generally appeared in just 1 size, which was smaller than or equal to the smallest size currently available.[26,27] This observation also holds for french fries, hamburgers, and soda, for which current sizes are 2 to 5 times larger than the originals.[25]

Our research also reveals indirect indicators of the increasing availability of larger food portions. In contrast to practices that were common just 15 to 25 years ago, food companies now use larger sizes as selling points (e.g., Double Gulp, Supersize); fast-food companies promote larger items with signs, staff pins, and placemats; manufacturers of diet meals such as Lean Cuisine and Weight Watchers frozen dinners advertise larger meal sizes; restaurant reviews refer to large portions;[28] and national chain restaurants promote large-size items directly on menus. Restaurants are using larger dinner plates, bakers are selling larger muffin tins, pizzerias are using larger pans, and fast-food companies are using larger drink and french fry containers.[25] Identical recipes for cookies and desserts in old and new editions of classic cookbooks such as *Joy of Cooking* specify fewer servings, meaning that portions are expected to be larger.[29,30] Another indicator of the trend toward larger portions is that automobile manufacturers have installed larger cup holders in newer models to accommodate the larger sizes of drink cups.[31] Overall, our observations indicate that the portion sizes of virtually all foods and beverages prepared for immediate consumption have increased and now appear typical.

Of interest is *when* portion sizes increased. We identified 181 products for which we were able to obtain dates of introduction. Our data suggest that the trend toward larger portion sizes began in the 1970s; portion sizes increased sharply in the 1980s and have continued to increase.

Discussion

Our data indicate that marketplace portions of foods that are major contributors of energy to US diets have increased significantly since the 1970s and exceed federal standards for dietary guidance and food labels. This trend can be attributed to multiple causes, some of them economic. Since the 1970s, the food service industry has grown larger, and people have been eating out more; marketing has become more concentrated, and larger numbers of new products have been introduced.[32] Widespread price competition has induced manufacturers to introduce larger items as a means to retain and expand market share; profits for most food items rise consistently when manufacturers increase product size.[33,34] From a marketing standpoint, oversized packages draw attention to a new product, as research has shown for beer, soft drinks, and fast food.[35–37] Concern about value also drives the food service industry to offer larger products; many restaurant owners report that customers want more food for their money,[38] and consumers increasingly choose restaurants on the basis of the sizes of food portions.[39] Large portions often seem like a bargain: 7-Eleven's 16-oz Gulp costs just under 5 cents/oz, but a 32-oz Big Gulp is 2.7 cents/oz.

Obviously, larger portions provide more calories. A 2.1-oz Butterfingers candy bar contains 270 kcal, whereas the 5.0-oz "Beast" supplies 680 kcal. The 7-Eleven Double Gulp, a 64-oz soda, contains nearly 800 kcal—an amount 10 times the size of a Coca-Cola when it was introduced[40] and calorically equivalent to more than one third of the energy requirement of large segments of the population.[41] Increased consumption of fast foods contributes to increased caloric intake;[42] this problem could well be made worse by the "supersizing" of menu items.[43] In the mid-1950s, McDonald's offered only 1 size of french fries; that size is now considered "Small" and is one third the weight of the largest size available in 2001. Today's "Large" weighs the same as the 1998 "Supersize," and the 2001 "Supersize" weighs nearly an ounce more. Since 1999, a McDonald's "Supersize" soda is nearly one third larger than the "Large." Notably, the sizes of chain fast-food portions in Europe are smaller than those in the United States. McDonald's "Extra Large" soda portions in London, Rome, and Dublin weigh the same as the US "Large." In 1998–1999, the largest order of french fries in the United States contained 610 calories,[44] whereas the largest size in the United Kingdom contained 446 calories.[45]

The trend toward larger portion sizes has occurred in parallel with other increases—in the availability of energy in the US food supply, in dietary intake of energy, and in the prevalence of overweight and obesity. Although parallel trends suggest a causal relationship, they also could reflect some external factor that affects these indicators, such as a decrease in energy expenditure that is too small to be measured by current methods for assessing activity levels.

Overall, our survey found that marketplace food portions are consistently larger than they were in the past as well as considerably larger than federal standard portion sizes. These observations suggest a need for greater attention to food portion size as a factor in energy intake and weight management. A recent survey reports that Americans tend to ignore serving size when they are attempting to maintain body weight.[46] Health authorities call for reducing the prevalence of overweight among Americans[47] and for public health approaches for doing so.[48] Public health efforts to explain the relationship of portion size to caloric intake, weight gain, and health might be helpful, as would efforts by federal agencies to make serving size definitions more consistent and comprehensible. The USDA has issued a statement that recognizes the gap between standard servings and typical portions[49] and could follow it with guidance materials. Portion size affects caloric balance, and educational and other public health programs are needed to address the effects of current food trends.

References

1. Mortality Statistics Branch, National Center for Health Statistics. "Update: Prevalence of Overweight Among Children, Adolescents, and Adults—United States, 1988–1994," *MMWR Morb Mortal Wkly Rep*, 1997; 46:199–202.

2. Flegal KM, Carroll MD, Kuczmarski RJ, Johnson CL. "Overweight and Obesity in the United States: Prevalence and Trends, 1960–1994," *Int J Obes*, 1998; 22:39–47. [PubMed]

3. Mokdad AH, Serdula MK, Dietz WH, Bowman BA, Marks JS, Koplan JP. "The Spread of the Obesity Epidemic in the United States, 1991–1998," *JAMA*, 1999; 282:1519–1522. [PubMed]

4. Mortality Statistics Branch, National Center for Health Statistics. "Physical Activity Trends—United States, 1990–1998," *MMWR Morb Mortal Wkly Rep*, 2001; 50:166–169. [PubMed]

5. *Physical Activity and Health: A Report of the Surgeon General.* Atlanta, Ga: US Dept of Health and Human Services, Centers for Disease Control and Prevention, 1996.

6. Life Sciences Research Office, Federation of American Societies for Experimental Biology. *Third Report on Nutrition Monitoring in the United States.* Vol 2. Washington, DC: US Government Printing Office, 1995.

7. US Department of Agriculture. "Data Tables: Results from USDA's 1994–96 Continuing Survey of Food Intakes by Individuals and 1994–96 Diet" and "Health Knowledge Survey," December 1997. Available at: http://www.barc.usda.gov/bhnrc/foodsurvey/home.htm. Accessed February 25, 1999.

8. Putnam JJ, Allshouse JE. *Food Consumption, Prices, and Expenditures.* Washington, DC: US Dept of Agriculture, Economic Research Service, 1999; Statistical Bulletin 965.

9. *US Trends in Eating Away From Home, 1982–1989.* Washington, DC: US Department of Agriculture, Economic Research Service; 1995; Statistical Bulletin 926.

10. Clauson A. "Share of Food Spending for Eating Out Reaches 47 Percent," *FoodReview*, 1999; 22:20–22.

11. Young LR, Nestle M. "Portion Sizes in Dietary Assessment: Issues and Policy Implications," *Nutr Rev*, 1995; 53:149–158. [PubMed]

12. Booth DA, Fuller J, Lewis V. "Human Control of Body Weight: Cognitive or Physiological? Some Energy Related Perceptions and Misperceptions." In: Cioffi LA, James WPT, Van Itallie TB, eds. *The Body Weight Regulatory System: Normal and Disturbed Mechanisms.* New York, NY: Raven Press, 1981:305–314.

13. Wansink B. "Can Package Size Accelerate Usage Volume?" *J Marketing*, 1996; 60:1–13.

14. Rolls BJ, Engell D, Birch LL. "Serving Portion Size Influences 5-Year-Old but Not 3-Year-Old Children's Food Intakes," *J Am Diet Assoc.* 2000; 100:232–234. [PubMed]

15. *Nutrition and Your Health: Dietary Guidelines for Americans,* 5th ed. Washington, DC: US Department of Agriculture, 2000; Home and Garden Bulletin 232.

16. *The Food Guide Pyramid,* rev ed. Washington, DC: US Dept of Agriculture, 1996; Home and Garden Bulletin 252.

17. Heimbach JT, Levy AS, Schucker RE. "Declared Serving Sizes of Packaged Foods, 1977–86," *Food Technol,* 1990; 44(6):82–90.

18. *USDA's Food Guide: Background and Development.* Hyattsville, Md: US Dept of Agriculture, Human Nutrition Information Service, 1992; Administrative Report 389.

19. US Food and Drug Administration. "Food Labeling: Serving Sizes," *Fed Regist,* 1993; 58:2229–2291.

20. Harnack LJ, Jeffery RW, Boutelle KN. "Temporal Trends in Energy Intake in the United States: an Ecologic Perspective," *Am J Clin Nutr,* 2000; 71:1478–1484. [PubMed]

21. "Top 50 Growth Chains," *Restaurant Business,* 1996; 95:51–122.

22. Lowe KD, Nicolas E. "The Top 400 Restaurant Concepts," *Restaurants Institutions,* 1997; 107(17).

23. Block G, Dresser CM, Hartman AM, Carroll MD. "Nutrient Sources in the American Diet: Quantitative Data from the NHANES II Survey," *Am J Epidemiol,* 1985; 122:27–40. [PubMed]

24. Subar AF, Krebs-Smith SM, Cook A, Kahle LL. "Dietary Sources of Nutrients Among US Adults, 1989 to 1991," *J Am Diet Assoc,* 1998; 98:537–547. [PubMed]

25. Young LR. *Portion Sizes in the American Food Supply: Issues and Implications* [dissertation]. New York, NY: New York University, 2000.

26. *The History of Anheuser-Busch Companies: A Fact Sheet.* St. Louis, Mo: Anheuser Busch, Inc, 1995.

27. *Bar Weight History.* Hershey, Pa: Hershey Foods Corporation, 1991.

28. *Zagat Survey 2000: New York City Restaurants.* New York, NY: Zagat Survey LLC, 1999.

29. Rombauer IS, Becker MR. *Joy of Cooking.* New York, NY: Penguin Books USA, 1964.

30. Rombauer IS, Becker MR, Becker E. *Joy of Cooking.* New York, NY: Scribner, 1997.

31. Siano J. "Garages Make Supersized SUV's Even Bigger for Superrich MVP's," *New York Times,* August 27, 2000:AU1.

32. Gallo AE. *The Food Marketing System in 1989*. Washington, DC: US Dept of Agriculture, Economic Research Service, 1990; Agriculture Information Bulletin 603.

33. Berry E. "Pricing Tactics and the Search for Profits," *Advertising Forum*, 1983; 4:12–13, 71–72.

34. Information Resources Inc. "At the Checkout: Big Sales for Big Products," *Wall Street Journal,* October 12, 1993:B1.

35. Phillips K. "Reprofitizing the Industry," *Beverage World,* September 1990:83–84.

36. Shapiro E. "Marketscan: Portions and Packages Grow Bigger and Bigger," *Wall Street Journal*, October 12, 1993:B1.

37. Gibson R, Coleman CY. "How Burger King Finally Became a Contender," *Wall Street Journal*, February 27, 1997:B1.

38. DiDomenico P. "Portion Size: How Much Is Too Much?" *Restaurants USA*, 1994; 14(6):18–21.

39. Carangelo C. "Why Are Americans So Fat?" *Food Management*, 1995; 30:63–68.

40. *Facts, Figures, and Features.* Atlanta, Ga: Coca-Cola Company, 1996.

41. National Research Council. *Recommended Dietary Allowances*, 10th ed. Washington, DC: National Academy Press, 1989.

42. Jeffery RW, French SA. "Epidemic Obesity in the United States: Are Fast Foods and Television Viewing Contributing?" *Am J Public Health*, 1998; 88:277–280. [PMC free article] [PubMed]

43. Hill JO, Peters JC. "Environmental Contributions to the Obesity Epidemic," *Science*, 1998; 280:1371–1374. [PubMed]

44. *McDonald's Nutrition Facts.* Oakbrook, Ill: McDonald's Corporation, 1999.

45. *Our Food. The Inside Story: Nutrition Analysis.* London, England: McDonald's Restaurants Ltd, 1998.

46. American Institute of Cancer Research. "New Survey Shows Americans Ignore Importance of Portion Size in Managing Weight." Available at: http://www.aicr.org. Accessed October 27, 2000.

47. *Healthy People 2010: Understanding and Improving Health*. Washington, DC: US Dept of Health and Human Services, Public Health Service, 2000.

48. Nestle M, Jacobson MF. "Halting the Obesity Epidemic: a Public Health Policy Approach," *Public Health Rep*, 2000; 115:12–24. [PMC free article] [PubMed]

49. Hogbin M, Shaw A, Anand RS. *Nutrition Insights: Food Portions and Servings. How Do They Differ?* Washington, DC: US Dept of Agriculture, 1999.

USDA Policies Reward Businesses for Selling Inexpensive, Unhealthy Food

David Wallinga

David Wallinga is a senior health advisor for the Natural Resources Defense Council (NRDC), a nonprofit environmental advocacy organization. He holds a bachelor's degree in political science from Dartmouth College, a master's degree in public affairs from Princeton University, and completed medical school at the University of Minnesota.

C hildhood obesity is epidemic, a problem of current disease but also of future costs. Treatment is expensive, is often ineffective, and fails to address worsening trends.[1] Primary prevention—preventing children from becoming overweight and obese in the first place—is the only long-term solution for this public health problem.

Record childhood obesity was foreseeable, given a modern "obesogenic" (to cause obesity) environment that discourages activity and encourages consumption of calorie-dense, nutrient-poor food,[2] combined with innate biological mechanisms that appear in many people to confer a propensity to accumulate and conserve energy.[3] Many good policy options exist for changing food availability, food prices, or food marketing—thereby influencing the food environment—at the local, state, and federal levels.[4] Nearly all such policies are aimed at the downstream, consumer end of the food chain. Policy makers and researchers have mostly overlooked the upstream links between obesity and policy determinants of what happens on the farm. Consequently, few have considered how changing agricultural policy might positively affect the availability and prices of food.

"Agricultural Policy And Childhood Obesity: A Food Systems and Public Health Commentary," by David Wallinga, *Health Affairs*, March 2010.

Two recent foundation-supported conferences[5,6] and a two-volume journal supplement[7] began to address this policy and research gap. The discussion in this paper reflects some common themes.

Calorie Excess and the American Food Supply

Research now links obesity promotion with the consumption of added fats, sugars, and refined grains and of the snacks, sweets, beverages, and fast foods in which they are prominent.

In 2002, US Department of Agriculture (USDA) researchers said that the prime factor behind soaring obesity rates was a 300-calorie jump, from 1985 to 2000, in how many calories the US food supply delivered to the average eater.[8] Of the extra calories, 24 percent came from added fats; 23 percent, from added sugars. Grains, mostly refined grains, accounted for 46 percent.[8]

Recently updated, the USDA data for 2007 show that Americans' average daily calorie intake is 400 calories higher than in 1985 and 600 calories higher than in 1970.[9] Among grains, corn calories (from corn flour, corn meal, hominy, and corn starch) led the way with a 191 percent increase since 1970. Added sugar intake—including cane and beet sugar, honey, syrups, and corn sweeteners—is up 14 percent over 1970 levels, but corn sweetener calories alone rose 359 percent to 246 calories per day.[9] By 2005–06, the average child drank 172 daily calories from sugar-sweetened beverages, including those sweetened with high-fructose corn syrup.[10]

Average daily calories from added fats and oils continue to rise, up 69 percent since 1970; a 260 percent calorie increase from salad and cooking oils is leading the way.[9] Of the fats and oils Americans eat, 70 percent are soy oil (mostly salad or cooking oils, plus baking and frying fats); another 8 percent are corn oil.[11]

American farms, not farms abroad, are the source for many of these extra fats, sugars, and calories. The United States is the world's largest corn producer, but it exports only around 20 percent of the total crop.[12] Almost 4.7 percent of the total corn crop gets diverted to produce high-fructose corn syrup.[13] The United States is also the world's largest soybean producer and exporter. It produced 20.6 billion pounds of soy oil in 2008, of which 93 percent was used domestically.[11]

Farmers and Agricultural Policy

Over the long term, what farmers grow is steered by agricultural policy. For more than a century, US policy has promoted US farmers' capacity to increase production, generally of the kind of commodities—corn, wheat, cotton, rice, milk, and later soybeans—that lend themselves to large-scale production, easy storage, and long-distance shipping.[14,15] Much of the public infrastructure to support farmers at the regional level (such as university research and extension services) came to be dominated by a focus on commodity and production agriculture.[16]

Growing the nation's agricultural capacity is generally recognized as a good thing. It serves national security as well as rural development needs, especially with a growing population. But production-oriented agriculture policy also has been promoted as important for nutrition. Early-twentieth-century research suggested that when hungry children were given diets higher in added fats and sugars, they grew. Following World War II, raising production of commodity crops and their associated fats and sugars was seen as an answer to undernutrition in the United States and throughout the world.[17] American commodity farmers continue to be reminded of their putative mission to "feed the world."[18]

US farmers responded fantastically to these policies, raising output 2.6 times from 1948 to 2002.[19] In 2009 they planted more than eighty-seven million corn acres, the second-highest total in sixty-two years. Yields of 150 bushels per acre or more are typical—600 percent higher than in 1920.[15]

Overproduction

Because they operate independently, commodity crop farmers have a long-established tendency to overproduce collectively. During the Great Depression, a production glut led to a predictable drop in prices and subsequent farm failures. Although there were fewer farmers, total farmland stayed the same as larger farms swallowed up smaller farms. What ensued were the first federal programs to manage the supply of agricultural commodities, both to stabilize prices and to sustain farm income. These programs largely worked over the next several decades, often at little or no net cost to the federal treasury. From 1965 to 1996, however, supply management programs were dismantled.

Starting in 1974, the USDA began implementing a federal "cheap food" policy that encouraged commodity farmers to produce as much as possible.[14] The case made by then Secretary of Agriculture Earl Butz was that by producing abundant and cheap commodity grains, US farmers would capture growing global markets.

Butz proved wrong. Instead of helping farmers prosper, persistent low prices (once again based on that tendency to overproduce) drove many commodity farmers out of business. When Congress passed the 1996 Farm Bill, however, it stripped away the last remnants of supply management and left all incentives for commodity overproduction in place. But when commodity prices continued to plunge, Congress was forced to pass a series of "emergency" payments to protect farmers from going out of business. By 2001, these payments had tripled to more than $20 billion per year,[14] and commodity crop prices had dropped 40 percent, on average.[20] In 2002, Congress made these subsidies permanent in a variety of different types of subsidies.

It must be noted that the advent of farm subsidies only followed policy failure and low prices. The latter created the need for the former. Cutting commodity subsidies therefore cannot be viewed as a quick fix for overproduction and low prices. Removing these subsidies, since they are not the root reason why commodity crops are overproduced in the first place, will not address the oversupply of cheap calories from these commodities. In the short term, what cutting commodity subsidies likely would do instead is to drive out of farming even more of the farmers who might otherwise have been offered policy incentives to produce a healthier long-term balance of commodities and other, noncommodity crops.

Outpaced by Science

A second problem with production-led agricultural policy is that it has not kept pace with the science. As a cheap calorie policy, it has been a success. Many more fats, sugars, and calories have been added to the American food supply. And foods high in fat, sugar, and calories, such as cooking oils, snacks, fast food, and sugared sodas, are some of the least expensive foods in the US food environment. Simply put, sweets and fats cost less, while many healthier foods cost more.[21] Unhealthy foods also are the most inflation-resistant part of the US diet.[22] Our analysis of USDA data shows that from 1985 to 2000, the inflation-adjusted price of carbonated soft drinks sank nearly 24 percent, while the prices of fresh fruit and vegetables rose 39 percent.[23]

What has changed since agricultural "cheap food" policies were put in place is that obesity has overtaken hunger as the most prevalent nutritional problem in children—too many calories, not too few. According to today's science, the quality of the calories produced by US agriculture may be at least as important as their quantity.

Fruit and Vegetable Deficits and the US Food Supply

Diets rich in fruits and vegetables can help manage weight and can lower risks for cancer and other chronic diseases, especially when they replace calorie-dense, nutrient-poor foods. Yet fewer than one in ten Americans meet the levels of fruit and vegetable consumption recommended under the latest calorie-specific healthy eating guidelines.[24,25] Despite the focus on nutrition education, fruit and vegetable consumption has stagnated or even declined in recent years.

USDA data indicate that the US food system supplies 24 percent fewer servings per person than the five daily vegetable servings recommended for a standard 2,000-calorie diet. Subtracting out starchy vegetables, the shortfall looks even worse. Only half of the recommended servings of dark green vegetables are available, along with one-third of the orange vegetables and one-quarter of the recommended legumes.[26] There is a supply shortfall in fruit as well. To meet recommended levels, Americans would need to increase daily fruit and vegetable consumption by 132 percent and 31 percent, respectively. But where that produce would come from is equally important, and largely determined by agricultural policy.

For supply to match an increase in consumption of any one fruit or vegetable group would require some combination of the following: (1) a rise in imports; (2) diversion of current exports to domestic consumption; and (3) an expansion of domestic production. One-quarter of fresh fruit consumption already is imported, and that percentage keeps rising. Raising imports does not seem to be an ideal long-term solution from several policy perspectives, including food safety worries, the carbon and costs embedded in shipping produce over long distances, and the national security concerns if other countries should prove unable or unwilling to ship their fruit and vegetables to the United States.

On the other hand, for US farmers to produce more fruit and vegetables nearer to consumers will require an agricultural policy that offers incentives to do so. The average American farmer is fifty-five years old, however, and fast approaching retirement.[27] Midscale farmers who cultivate 100–500 acres are the ones best positioned to offer a more diverse set of foods, including fruits and vegetables, to a more local market and have the flexibility to increase production to a larger scale.[28] Midsize farms are disappearing most rapidly. As farm numbers shrink, remaining farms get bigger. In the Farm Belt especially, larger farms generally produce one or two commodities, such as corn or soybeans, and nothing else. Their entire experience and capital investment is devoted to that single purpose.

US agricultural policy generally has not offered incentives or supported farmers to grow fruits and vegetables. Their production does not qualify for direct payments under Title I of the Farm Bill. In fact, farmers who would like to receive support under these programs have been explicitly prohibited from planting fruits and vegetables.[29]

Agricultural Policy and the Food Environment

Childhood obesity is a problem growing three times faster than adult obesity.[30] The specter of ever-rising future costs, death, and disease from today's ever-worsening trends demands bold action. Yet policy makers have had a blind spot with respect to the links between US farm policy and worsening obesity. America spends $147 billion a year on obesity-related illness. Policy makers fail to connect this spending, for example, to $21 billion in Farm Bill spending to support commodity crop production in one year (2005) alone. Expected Farm Bill spending over the next decade will total in the hundreds of billions of dollars. The next Farm Bill is in 2012. Policy decisions made now will determine whether these public investments are to be effective at helping to reverse, rather than to worsen, obesity trends.

The complex, messy, obesogenic US food environment has been decades in the making. Changing it will not be easy, because the "set point" or defaults are woven so tightly and broadly into the fabric of our food system and its policies. Policy makers would be prudent to guard against putative quick fixes—such as the elimination of subsidy payments to commodity farmers—to the system's longstanding, multidimensional problems.

As noted earlier, doing away with these particular subsidies would not address the underlying reasons—including a national "cheap food" policy—why farmers overproduce commodity crops and underproduce healthy fruits and vegetables in the first place. Further, because farmers' livelihoods and decisions have been predicated on these policies, a quick reversal would exact considerable harm and likely would further erode the already too limited supply of US farmers essential for growing the fruits and vegetables needed for healthier diets in the future.

A successful redesign of the food environment will likely require a long-term commitment to mutually supportive interventions, at multiple levels (local, state, and federal) from farm to plate, to effect change in food availability, relative prices, and marketing, complemented by nutrition education.[24] One component of this redesign could include reinstating programs to manage the oversupply of commodity crops and calories, combined with support for new farmers as well as for existing farmers who want to transition away from exclusive production of commodity crops. Upstream changes to agricultural policy are critical, but in the end are only one among many needed changes.

Near-Term Policy Changes

Yet small, incremental changes to the calorie-dense food supply could have outsize impacts. Over ten years, an extra 130 calories per day (less than what is in a twelve-ounce can of sugared soda) can spell the difference between a young child on her way to obesity and one who is not.[31] We suggest the following as doable, near-term policy steps.

Seek Executive Leadership

At another critical juncture in the nation's nutritional health, the 1969 White House Conference on Food, Nutrition, and Health was convened. This landmark effort ultimately gave rise to expansion of the food stamp, food labeling, and school lunch programs.[32] The time may be now for renewed executive-branch leadership to bring together disparate health and agriculture communities around food policy, among other upstream determinants of childhood obesity.

Integrate Food and Health Analysis
Obesity is a systems problem, inexorably related to the equally complex and problematic food system. There is no single entity to inform policy makers broadly about the health impacts, including on childhood obesity, of the entire food system.

With fragmented authority and expertise across a dizzying number of federal agencies (USDA, Food and Drug Administration, Environmental Protection Agency, Centers for Disease Control and Prevention, Health and Human Services, Consumer Product Safety Commission, National Institutes of Health, and so on), this perhaps is no surprise. Something like the United Kingdom's Food Commission is needed. That commission is a nongovernmental organization that looks beyond "stable to table" analyses to link food production policies with nutrition and health policies.[33]

Support Farmers as Anti-Obesity Partners
American farmers have proved adept at responding to the policy conditions determined for them. Indeed, farmers are essential allies in the fight against obesity. If the nation is to get serious about making fruits, vegetables, and other healthy food more accessible, policy makers need to offer at least as much research, financial, and other support to domestic farmers of these crops as has been done for commodity crop growers for decades. Policy interventions could include recruiting and training new farmers; grants or financing on favorable terms for new farmers, including for land acquisition and for farmers moving from commodity to other production; and allowing fruit and vegetable farmers to participate in any commodity programs of the Farm Bill.

Invest in Forward-Looking Research
The critical research program ("title") of the 2012 Farm Bill will set the direction of agricultural health and innovation for years to come. Given the challenges of greater climate uncertainty, coming water scarcity, development pressure on prime croplands, and obesity, America needs a research agenda to inform what diverse mix of crops and farming methods can best meet the nation's health

and other needs, sustainably. The National Institutes of Health and other health agencies' research programs could better complement USDA research initiatives in realizing this goal.

Codify Healthier Commodity Food Programs

Many surplus commodities produced under Farm Bill programs make their way into federal child nutrition programs, such as the National School Lunch and Breakfast Programs, where they often have not conformed to the USDA's own dietary guidelines for healthy eating. The most effective policy for better aligning commodities with students' nutritional needs is to raise nutrition standards for all food served in these programs. Already positive USDA steps in this direction should be codified and incorporated into this year's reauthorization of the Child Nutrition Act.

Conclusion

Agricultural production affects nutrition, obesity, and health. Agricultural policy helps determine not only what farmers grow, but what people eat, how easy it is to access that food, and what they pay for it. All too soon, the nation will confront the need for a new Farm Bill. Its contents ought to be as great a concern for urban eaters as for rural farmers, and as much a priority for health policy makers as for agriculture policy makers. We need much more than another Farm Bill. We need a Healthy Food, Healthy Farm Bill.

Notes

1. Brownell KD , Warner KE. "The Perils of Ignoring History: Big Tobacco Played Dirty and Millions Died. How Similar Is Big Food?" *Milbank Q,* 2009; *87* (1): 259–94.

2. Brownell KD , Schwartz MB , Puhl RM , Henderson KE , Harris JL . "The Need for Bold Action to Prevent Adolescent Obesity . *J Adolesc Health*, 2009; 45 Suppl 3: S8–17.

3. *Foresight. Tackling Obesities: Future Choices.* London,UK: U.K. Government Office of Science, 2007.

4. National Conference of State Legislatures. *Healthy Community Design and Access to Healthy Food Legislation Database* [Internet]. Denver, CO: NCSL [cited Jan 15 2010]. Available from: http://www.ncsl.org/IssuesResearch

/EnvironmentandNaturalResources/HealthyCommunityDesignandAccessto
HealthyFoo/tabid/13227/Default.aspx.

5. "Food Systems and Public Health Conference: Linkages to Achieve Healthier Diets and Healthier Communities." Airlie Center, Warrenton, VA, 2009; April 1–3. In: "Conference Agenda: Food Systems and Public Health: Linkages to Achieve Healthier Diets and Healthier Communities," *J Hunger Environ Nutr*, 2009; *4* (3–4): 486–8.

6. "Conference Summary: The Wingspread Conference on Childhood Obesity, Healthy Eating, and Agricultural Policy" [Internet]. Healthy Eating Research Program, Robert Wood Johnson Foundation and Institute for Agriculture and Trade Policy, Racine, WI, 2007; Mar [cited 2010 Jan 20]. Available from: http://www.healthyeatingresearch.org/images/stories/her_wingspread/1wingspreadsummary.pdf.

7. Story M, Hamm MW, Wallinga D, eds. "Special Issue: Food Systems and Public Health—Linkages to Achieve Healthier Diets and Healthier Communities," *J Hung Environ Nutr*, 2009; *4* (3–4): 219–508.

8. The USDA treats these data, adjusted for exports, imports, and food losses, as a proxy for consumption. See Putnam J, Allshouse J, Kantor LS. "US Per Capita Food Supply Trends: More Calories, Refined Carbohydrates, and Fats," *Food Rev*, 2002; *25* (3): 2–15.

9. Economic Research Service. *Loss Adjusted Food Availability* [database on the Internet]. Washington, DC: US Department of Agriculture; updated February 2009 [cited 10 Jan 2010]. Available from: http://www.ers.usda.gov/Data/FoodConsumption/FoodGuideIndex.htm.

10. Brownell KD, Farley T, Willett WC, Popkin BM, Chaloupka FJ, Thompson JW, et al. "The Public Health and Economic Benefits of Taxing Sugar-Sweetened Beverages," *N Engl J Med*, 2009; *361*(16): 1599–1605.

11. American Soybean Association. *Soy Stats 2009* [Internet]. St. Louis, MO: American Soybean Association; [cited 15 Jan 2010]. Available from: http://www.soystats.com/2009/Default-frames.htm.

12. Economic Research Service. *Briefing Rooms: Corn* [Internet]. Washington, DC: US Department of Agriculture; [cited 10 Jan 2010]. Available from:http://www.ers.usda.gov/briefing/Corn/.

13. Economic Research Service. *Briefing Room—Sugar and Sweeteners: Background* [Internet]. Washington, DC: US Department of Agriculture; [cited 15 Jan 2010]. Available from: http://www.ers.usda.gov/Briefing/sugar/background.htm#hfcs

14. Ray DE , De La Torre Ugarte DG , Tiller KJ. *Rethinking US Agricultural Policy: Changing Course to Secure Farmer Livelihoods Worldwide.* Knoxville, TN: University of Tennessee, Agricultural Policy Analysis Center, 2003.

15. Wallinga D. "Today's Food System: How Healthy Is It?" *J Hung Environ Nutr*, 2009; *4* (3): 251–81.

16. National Research Council. *Publicly Funded Agricultural Research and the Changing Structure of US Agriculture*. Washington, DC: National Academies Press, 2002.

17. Lang T. "European Agricultural Policy: Is Health the Missing Link?" *Eurohealth*, 2004; *10* (1): 4–8.

18. Voice of Agriculture. *Stallman to Ag Critics: Circumstances Have Changed* [Internet]. Washington, DC: American Farm Bureau, 2010 [cited 2010 Jan 20]. Available from: http://www.fb.org/index.php?fuseaction=newsroom .newsfocus&year=2010&file=nr0110.html.

19. Ball E. "Ag Productivity Drives Output Growth," *Amber Waves* [serial on the Internet], 2005 Jun [cited 2010 Jan 20]. Available from: http://www.ers.usda.gov /AmberWaves/June05/Findings/AgProductivity.htm.

20. Philpott T. *The 2007 Farm—and Food—Bill* [Internet]. Backgrounder, Oakland, CA: Food First/Institute for Food and Development Policy, 2006 Oct 27 [cited 2010 Jan 20]. Available from: http://www.foodfirst.org/backgrounders/fall2006.

21. Drewnowski A, Specter SE. "Poverty and Obesity: The Role of Energy Density and Energy Costs," *Am J Clin Nutr*, 2004; *79*: 6–16.

22. Monsivais P, Drewnowski A. "The Rising Cost of Low-Energy-Density Foods," *J Am Diet Assoc,* 2007; *107* (12): 2071–6.

23. Wallinga D, Schoonover H, Muller M. "Considering the Contribution of US Agricultural Policy to the Obesity Epidemic: Overview and Opportunities," *J Hung Environ Nutr*, 2009; *4* (1): 3–19.

24. Kimmons J, Gillespie C, Seymour J, Serdula M, Blanck HM. "Fruit and Vegetable Intake Among Adolescents and Adults in the United States: Percentage Meeting Individualized Recommendations," *Medscape J Med*, 2009; *11* (1): 26. Medline.

25. US Department of Health and Human Services and US Department of Agriculture. *Dietary Guidelines for Americans, 2005*, 6th ed. [Internet]. Washington, DC: US Government Printing Office; 2005 [cited 18 Jan 2010]. Available from: http://www.health.gov/DietaryGuidelines/dga2005/document /default.htm.

26. Buzby JC, Wells HF, Vocke G. *Possible Implications for US Agriculture from Adoption of Select Dietary Guidelines* [Internet]; Report no. 31. Washington, DC: US Department of Agriculture, Economic Research Service, 2006 [cited 14 Jan 2010]. Available from: http://www.ers.usda.gov/Publications/ERR31/.

27. National Agricultural Statistics Service. *Demographics of US Farm Operators* [Internet]. Washington, DC: US Department of Agriculture, [cited 14 Jan 2010]. Available from: http://www.agcensus.usda.gov/Publications/2002/Other_Analysis /index.asp.

28. Kirschenmann F, Stevenson S, Buttel F, Lyson T, Duffy M, eds. *Why Worry About Agriculture of the Middle?* [Internet]. White Paper. Agriculture of the Middle Project, 2004 [cited 2010 Jan 16]. Available from: http://www.agofthemiddle.org /papers/whitepaper2.pdf.

29. Economic Research Service. *Base Acreage and Planting Restrictions Under the 2002 Farm Act*[Internet]. Washington, DC: US Department of Agriculture [cited 16 Jan 2010]. Available from: http://www.ers.usda.gov/publications/err30/err30b.pdf.

30. Ogden CL, Carroll MD, Flegal KM. "High Body Mass Index for Age Among US Children and Adolescents, 2003–2006," *JAMA*, 2008; *299* (20): 2401–5. Crossref, Medline, Google Scholar.

31. Wang YC, Gortmaker GL, Sobol AM, Kuntz KM. "Estimating the Energy Gap Among US Children: a Counterfactual Approach," *Pediatrics*, 2006; *118* (6): 1721–33.

32. National Nutrition Summit 2000. *1969 Conference on Food, Nutrition, and Health* [Internet]. Bethesda, MD: National Institutes of Health, 2 Dec 1969 [cited2010 Jan 29]. Available from: http://www.nns.nih.gov/1969/full_report/PDFcontents.htm.

33. Lobstein T. "Food Policies: a Threat to Health?" *Proc Nutr Soc*, 2002; *61* (4): 579–86.

Government Intervention in the Food Market Prevents a Balanced Food Supply

Jeffrey A. Tucker

Jeffrey A. Tucker is the Editorial Director of the American Institute for Economic Research. He writes on economics, promotes anarcho-capitalism, and publishes libertarian books.

Every health nut will tell you the reason why the US food market is such a mess. It's fast food and corporate farming. We need to get back to local food and organics, they say. And no processed foods ever.

Let's look more closely, based on an experience I had just today.

The waiter in this airport bar walked by carrying huge plates of food, piled high with fries and burgers on puffy golden buns, then another with a gleaming plate of chicken wings covered with barbecue sauce and along with side dishes of more fries, then another with a massive pasta dish covered in white cheese, followed by another carrying a gigantic wedge of chocolate cake topped with ice cream and a caramel sauce.

My goodness, this place is generous with portions!

So it came time for me to order. I picked the catch of the day, which was Mahi Mahi, along with some asparagus and some slaw. Sounds great! The other plates were $15. Mine was $29. Ouch. That's annoying but sometimes you have to put aside price to get what sounds right.

But when it came, my plate looked nothing like the other plates of food around me. It had a very small piece of fish. There were six asparagus spears. The slaw was fine but limited. There was a small relish for the fish. And that was it.

I ate it all in about six minutes. There goes thirty bucks down the drain. And I look around and see happy customers chowing down on glorious plates of food, dumping ketchup (sugar) over everything, delighting in the excess.

Good for them. Sad for me. Or maybe not.

The Science Was Wrong

If you pay even the slightest attention to all the latest research on diet, you know of the emerging consensus. The famous "food pyramid" of the 1970s, along with the dietary recommendations by the federal government, were completely wrong. The war on fat, the huge emphasis on grains (and corn!), the minimal place of fresh vegetables and fruits, the attack on eggs and meat, and all the rest of what was once conventional science, seems to be melting away.

Meanwhile, the American obesity problem, along with all associated health issues, is out of control. The obesity rate has doubled since the 1980s. It is the second leading cause of premature death. Some data show that nearly a third of Americans can be classified as obese. Even our pets are developing an obesity problem. Maybe they are eating what we are eating.

You don't have to read the science to know this. Stay abroad for a few weeks and return to the states, and you notice, perhaps for the first time, that Americans look, ahem, different from other people in the world. You also notice that the food choice—I don't mean at farmer's markets or stores with a philosophy but rather the mainstream fare—is very different in the US.

For example, I've spent the last several days in the Caribbean. The food is fresh and healthy, with all kinds of fruits and delicious veggies plus wonderful meats. Breads are there but play a minor role in the overall offerings. Desserts are yummy but not that sweet. The same is true everywhere I've been lately, outside the US.

In the US, by contrast, the diet is driven by the market but it's a deeply distorted market, where the poor choices get the subsidies and the better choices are left to face competitive cold winds.

The *Economist* explains "American farm subsidies are egregiously expensive, harvesting $20 billion a year from taxpayers' pockets. Most of the money goes to big, rich farmers producing staple commodities such as corn and soyabeans in states such as Iowa."

The Centers for Disease Control [and Prevention] actually funded a massive study on the whole topic. The question: What is the link between the foods that make us fat and sick and the foods that are subsidized by the federal government? The result is just about as clear as empirical science can be.

> Among the justifications for the 1973 US Farm Bill was to assure consumers a plentiful supply of food at reasonable prices. Four decades later, the US population is burdened by substantial obesity and cardiometabolic disease. Suboptimal diet quality is a leading factor associated with death and disability in the United States. Specifically, diets that are high in calories, saturated fats, salt, and sugars but low in fruits and vegetables have been implicated in the development of cardiometabolic risk factors (obesity or adiposity, elevated blood pressure, elevated lipid levels, and diabetes) and diseases.

Why Does this Matter?

Many people who are curious about this relationship—I would even say nearly all!—explain the whole problem as tracing to "corporate farming" and "processed foods." Or to put it in brief: fast food. The problem here is that this is imprecise and comes close to blaming industrial progress itself for the problem.

The real root is deeper. It is not corporations or technology. They have made it possible to feed 7.6 billion people, in complete defiance of every Malthusian prediction of disaster dating back centuries. Nor is it the method or speed of delivery. The core of the problem is the massive price distortions in the market that have been brought about by government intervention.

The power of the corn lobby, for example, is legendary. And mixed with that is the power of the sugar lobby, which keeps out imported sugar that would sell for half as much as we pay at the store, thereby incentivizing producers to seek out a substitute in corn, which turns out to make us fatter, thereby panicking do-gooders who try to ban products and limit consumption, so that our bad health will stop driving up health-insurance rates.

I don't even need to look at the ingredients of the dessert that passed by my table to know the high likelihood that the cake, ice cream, sauce, and whipped topping contains corn at all levels. It's actually not easy to find any mainstream American food that is not built from some corn product. Take a tour of your local convenience store and look at the ingredients: observe the ever-malleable presence of corn. The food you seem to be looking at is not the food you are eating.

Blame Not the Market

The market is being blamed, once again, for a problem that traces to government itself. Remarkably, all of this has happened only since the 1970s, before which there was no such thing as high-fructose corn syrup, to say nothing of corn-based gasoline. It's one intervention piled on top of another one.

Foreign peoples find all of this mystifying. Indeed it is, until you look more deeply and see just how important the grain states are in winning elections. It turns out that the main and most valuable products generated by all this strange bad-food activity are political careers.

It's for this reason that we have corn coming out of our ears. We have french fries stacked to the heavens. We have breads, grains, and corn syrup taking over our lives, stuffed in our animals, and porking us all up to the point of rampant disease—all made available at absurdly cheap prices to the point that eating a healthy diet seems economically irrational.

Now, to be sure, this is, as they say, a "first world problem." For most of our 150,000 years of scraping by, humans have mostly struggled to get a bite to eat every day. It's the number one problem that has defined our existence. That we've somehow solved this problem is amazing. That we've replaced that old problem with a new problem—eating too much of the wrong kind of food—is extremely strange.

If we had a genuine free market in food—and the market is doing its best with the Amazon acquisition of Whole Foods—we would also likely see a greater alignment between what is affordable and what is actually good food for human consumption. It would be nice at least to be able to test this, starting with an end to the farm program.

CHAPTER 3

Does the Industrial Food Complex Harm the Environment?

Agriculture's Industrialization Currently Relies on Fossil Fuels

Richard Heinberg and Michael Bomford

Richard Heinberg is a senior fellow at the Post Carbon Institute. His journalistic work focuses on energy, the economy, and the environment. Michael Bomford, PhD, teaches in the Sustainable Agriculture and Food Systems program at Kwantien Polytechnic University. He focuses on sustainable farming.

During the past century world annual agricultural production has more than tripled. This unprecedented achievement in humanity's quest for food security and abundance was largely made possible by the development of chemical fertilizers, pesticides, and herbicides; new hybrid crop varieties; the application of irrigation in arid regions; and the introduction of powered farm machinery.

Central to most of these strategies for intensifying farm productivity were fossil fuels, especially oil and natural gas. Natural gas provides the hydrogen and energy used to produce most nitrogen fertilizers, and both gas and oil are the sources for other agricultural chemicals, including pesticides and herbicides. Meanwhile, oil fuels most farm machinery (often including irrigation pumps), and has enabled growth in the scale and distance of transportation of crop inputs and outputs. Today, food items are shipped worldwide and enormous quantities of food are routinely transported from places of abundance to sites of scarcity, enabling cities to be built in deserts.

This application of fossil fuels to the food system has supported a human population growing from fewer than two billion at the turn of the twentieth century to nearly seven billion today. In the process, the way we feed ourselves has changed profoundly.

Richard Heinberg and Michael Bomford, "The Food and Farming Transition: Toward a Post-Carbon Food System," (Sebastopol, Calif., USA: Post Carbon Institute, 2009); online at https://www.postcarbon.org/publications/food-and-farming-transition/.

Particularly in industrialized nations, the food system has become more articulated (it has more basic components) and more centralized. Today in most countries, farmers make up a smaller proportion of the population, and they typically work larger parcels of land. They also typically sell their harvest to a distributor or processor, who then sells packaged food products to a wholesaler, who in turn sells these products to chains of supermarkets. The ultimate consumer of the food is thus several steps removed from the producer, and food systems in most nations or regions have become dominated by a few giant multinational seed companies, agricultural chemicals corporations, and farm machinery manufacturers, as well as food wholesalers, distributors, and supermarket chains. In the US, the process of getting food from the farm to the plate uses over four times as much energy as farming.

Farming has also become far more mechanized. Fuel-fed machines plow, plant, harvest, sort, process, and deliver foods. The near-elimination of human and animal muscle-power from the food system has reduced production costs and increased labor productivity—which means that there is need for fewer farmers as a proportion of the population.

Farm inputs have also changed. A century ago, farmers saved seeds from year to year, while soil amendments were likely to come from the farm itself in the form of animal manures (though in many instances manures were imported from off-site). Farmers also bought basic implements, plus some ancillary materials such as lubricants.

Today's industrial farmer relies on an array of packaged products (seeds, fertilizers, pesticides, herbicides, feed, antibiotics), as well as fuels, powered machines, and spare parts. The annual cash outlays for these can be dauntingly large, requiring farmers to take out substantial loans.

From an energy perspective, industrialization presents a paradoxical reversal. Before the industrial revolution, farming and forestry were society's primary net producers of energy. Today the food system is a net user of energy in virtually every nation; this is especially so in industrial countries, where each calorie of food energy produced and brought to the table represents an average investment of about 7.3 calories of energy inputs.

It has been possible to create and maintain net energy-consuming food systems only because of the development by society of ways to extract and use fossil fuels, a one-time-only gift from nature to humanity representing sources of energy of unprecedented cheapness and abundance.

The benefits of industrial (that is to say, fossil fuel-based) food production and distribution are easy to see: our modern food system delivers products that are themselves cheap and abundant. In 2005, for example, the average US family spent less than 12 percent of income on food, whereas 50 years ago that percentage was about twice as high. Exotic foods are widely available in supermarkets, whose shelves display thousands of distinct food products. Famine, which used to be common throughout the world, is banished from most countries. Hunger, where it still exists, is nearly always due to an inability to afford food, rather than absolute scarcity.

A Mixed Blessing

But this enormous benefit has come at a cost. Out of all human activities, agriculture has arguably been the source of greatest human impact on the environment. Fertilizer runoff has led to the proliferation of oceanic dead zones fanning out from the mouths of rivers; the search for more arable land has driven widespread deforestation; irrigation has caused the salinization of soils; pesticide and herbicide pollution of air and water has adversely affected the health of humans as well as thousands of plant and animal species; and the simplification of ecosystems for the production of monocrops has exacerbated the ongoing loss of habitat for birds, amphibians, mammals, and beneficial insects.

Agriculture also contributes to climate change—principally through soil degradation, which releases carbon sequestered in soil into the atmosphere as carbon dioxide, but also through the combustion of fossil fuels. Climate change in turn adversely impacts agriculture through extreme weather events, altered seasons, and changing precipitation patterns.

Meanwhile, the industrialization of the food system has lowered food quality. Hundreds of millions of poor, middle-class, and even wealthy individuals in industrialized nations suffer from malnutrition, often hidden and sometimes paradoxically accompanied by obesity resulting from the consumption of highly processed foods low in essential nutrients. Four of the leading causes of death in these nations—heart disease, stroke, Type 2 diabetes, and cancer—are chronic diseases linked to diet.

Industrialized agriculture has reshaped the global economy in ways that have helped some but hurt many others. Poor farmers who cannot afford machines, fuels, and commercial farm inputs often find themselves at a disadvantage in the global food economy. Compounding this are agricultural policies in industrialized food-exporting countries that subsidize domestic producers and dump surpluses in poor nations (thus creating further economic disadvantage for smaller producers).

The result has been a systematic driving out of millions of small producers annually, the prioritization (in less-industrialized countries) of production for export, and the creation of a landless poor urban class (whose immediate ancestors were subsistence farmers) that is chronically malnourished and hungry.

At the same time, the centralized and mechanized fossil fuel-based food system has had a more subtle but nevertheless significant psycho-social impact. Modern city dwellers are increasingly alienated from the sources of their food, and so they purchase packaged and highly processed food with little understanding of the health consequences of its consumption or the environmental costs incurred in its manufacture. These latter trends have provoked a response in the form of the burgeoning local food and Slow Food movements, which seek to rebuild the connections between food, culture, and place.

However, the largest potential cost resulting from the industrialization of agriculture may lie in the extreme vulnerability of the entire system to global fossil fuel depletion.

The Depletion Dilemma

The inevitability of fuel supply problems is axiomatic, given the fact that oil and natural gas are non-renewable, with existing reserves constantly being depleted. Global oil discoveries have been declining since the 1960s (the peak year for discovery of new oilfields was 1964). The US passed its moment of peak production in 1970, and since then many more nations have entered the decline phase of their oil production history.

Moreover, acute supply disruptions are increasingly likely over the short term given the economic and geopolitical challenges accompanying the current global economic downturn.

Oil analysts dispute the likely timing of the inevitable global oil production peak, but even resource optimists concede that total non-OPEC crude oil production will begin its historic and terminal decline within the next few years, so that whatever spare production capacity remains will be concentrated in a few countries within a politically unstable geographic region.

The oil price spike of 2008 is an instructive harbinger of what is to come. Throughout 2006, 2007, and early 2008, world demand for oil grew, but supplies remained stagnant. Then, following a price surge during the first half of 2008, economic impacts from high fuel costs together with the unfolding of the world financial crisis caused oil demand to subside quickly and significantly. Oil prices plummeted in response.

The 2008 oil price spike contributed to a near-simultaneous doubling of food commodity prices; other causes included poor harvests due to drought and other adverse weather conditions in several key countries, growing demand by expanding Asian economies, commodity speculation, the decline in the value of the dollar, and the growth in biofuel production. As a result of these high food prices, more than 30 nations saw food riots in late 2008.

The use of synthetic nitrogen fertilizer, made primarily with natural gas, peaked in the late 1980s in the industrialized world, but continues to increase steadily in less-industrialized nations, leading to continued growth in world demand. Fertilizer prices spiked with oil prices in 2008, reflecting the fertilizer industry's dependence on cheap energy.

Higher fuel costs hit not just farmers—who have to buy fuel for their tractors, as well as fertilizers and other agricultural chemicals made from oil and natural gas—but the entire food system: the cost of processing, packaging, and shipping food rose, making food costs a significant contributor to overall economic inflation.

An indirect impact of oil prices on food production has come by way of the push to expand biofuels production. As petroleum has grown more costly, governments have offered increased subsidies and other incentives for turning biomass into fuel. This inevitably makes food more expensive. Even non-fuel crops such as wheat are affected, as farmers replace wheat fields with biofuel feedstock crops such as maize, rapeseed, or soy.

The price spike of 2008, whose full impacts have yet to be calculated, was not an isolated event but the beginning of an inevitable trend. Higher oil prices and oil shortages will hit poor farmers first. Already, many farmers in Africa are seeing yields plummet as they try to maintain the industrial methods they have been trained in (by the World Bank, IMF, and various aid agencies) while withholding the petrochemical inputs they can no longer afford.

Perhaps most frightening of all are the implications of fuel scarcity for food distribution: if high fuel prices, or a cut-off in supplies due to a sudden geopolitical event, were to keep trucks from delivering food to supermarkets (as nearly happened in Britain in 2000 and again in 2008 due to truckers' strikes), the shelves would quickly empty. Disruptions to the energy-intensive food processing, packaging, and preservation segments of our food system could be equally troublesome. While inevitable higher prices for petroleum are worrisome, protracted absolute scarcity would be a nightmare almost beyond contemplation.

A Survival Strategy

The only way to avert a food crisis resulting from oil and natural gas price hikes and supply disruptions while also reversing agriculture's contribution to climate change is to proactively and methodically remove fossil fuels from the food system. The methods for doing so are outlined in more detail throughout the remainder of this document.

It must be borne in mind that the removal of fossil fuels from the food system is inevitable: maintenance of the current system is simply not an option over the long term. Only the amount of time available for the transition process, and the strategies for pursuing it, should be matters for debate.

Given the degree to which the modern food system has become dependent on fossil fuels, many proposals for de-linking food and fossil fuels are likely to appear radical. However, efforts toward this end must be judged not by the degree to which they preserve the status quo, but by their likely ability to solve the fundamental challenge that will face us: the need to feed a global population of seven billion with a diminishing supply of fuels available to fertilize, plow, and irrigate fields and to harvest and transport crops. Additionally, it should be noted that it is in farmers' interest to reduce their dependence on fossil fuels, as this builds resilience against future resource scarcity and price volatility.

While many tactics can be explored (and many will be place-specific in any case), some of the necessary outlines of a general transition strategy are already clear:

- In general, farmers can no longer assume that products derived from petroleum and natural gas (chiefly diesel, gasoline, synthetic fertilizers, and synthetic pesticides) will remain relatively available and affordable in the future—and thus should change their business plans accordingly.

- Farmers should move toward regenerative fertility systems that build humus and sequester carbon in soils, thus contributing to solving climate change rather than exacerbating it.
- Farmers should reduce their use of pesticides in favor of integrated systems of pest management that rely primarily on biological, cultural, and physical controls.
- More of the renewable energy that will power society can and must be generated on farms. Wind and biomass production, in particular, can provide farmers with added income while also powering farm operations.
- Nations and regions must deliberately reduce the energy needed to transport food by relocalizing their food systems. This will entail support for local producers and for local networks that bring producers and consumers together. More efficient modes of transportation, such as ships and trains, must replace less efficient modes, such as trucks and planes.
- The end of the fossil fuel era must also be reflected in a change of diet and consumption patterns among the general population, with a preference for food that is locally grown, that is in season, and that is less processed. A shift away from energy-intensive, meat-centered diets should be encouraged.
- With less fuel available to power agricultural machinery, the world will need many more farmers. But for farmers to succeed, current agricultural policies that favor larger-scale production and production for export will need to change, while policies that support small-scale subsistence farming, gardening, and agricultural co-ops must be formulated and put in place—both by international institutions such as the World Bank, and also by national and regional governments.

If this transition is undertaken proactively and intelligently, there could be many side benefits—more careers in farming, more protection for the environment, less soil erosion, a revitalization of rural culture, and significant improvements in public health. Some of this transformation will inevitably be driven by market forces, led simply by the rising price of fossil fuels. However, without planning the transition may be wrenching and destructive, since market forces acting alone could bankrupt farmers while leaving consumers with few or no options for securing food supplies.

[…]

Industrial Farms Pollute the Air

The Earth Institute

The Earth Institute at Columbia University seeks to advance the knowledge of earth science and to use that knowledge to promote better environmental policy. The institute includes scientists, economists, policy experts, researchers, professors, and students at over two dozen research centers.

A new study says that emissions from farms outweigh all other human sources of fine-particulate air pollution in much of the United States, Europe, Russia and China. The culprit: fumes from nitrogen-rich fertilizers and animal waste that combine in the air with industrial emissions to form solid particles—a huge source of disease and death. The good news: if industrial emissions decline in coming decades, as most projections say, fine-particle pollution will go down even if fertilizer use doubles as expected. The study appears this week in the journal *Geophysical Research Letters*.

Agricultural air pollution comes mainly in the form of ammonia, which enters the air as a gas from heavily fertilized fields and livestock waste. It then combines with pollutants from combustion—mainly nitrogen oxides and sulfates from vehicles, power plants and industrial processes—to create tiny solid particles, or aerosols, no more than 2.5 micrometers across, about 1/30 the width of a human hair. The particles can penetrate deep into lungs, causing heart or pulmonary disease; a 2015 study in the journal *Nature* estimates they cause at least 3.3 million deaths each year globally.

The new study is not the first to flag agricultural pollution; many regional studies, especially in the United States, have shown it as a prime source of fine-particulate precursors. However, the study is perhaps the first to look at the phenomenon worldwide,

"A Major Source of Air Pollution: Farms," Earth Institute, Columbia University, June 16, 2016. Reprinted by permission.

and to project future trends. It shows that more than half the aerosol ingredients in much of the eastern and central United States come from farming. In Europe and China, the effect is even stronger. The aerosols form mainly downwind of farming areas, in densely populated places where farm emissions combine through a series of chemical reactions with those of cars, trucks and other sources.

"This is not against fertilizer—there are many places, including Africa, that need more of it," said lead author Susanne Bauer, an atmospheric scientist at Columbia University's Center for Climate Systems Research and the NASA Goddard Institute for Space Studies. "We expect population to go up, and to produce more food, we will need more fertilizer."

The fact that agricultural emissions must combine with other pollutants to make aerosols "is good news," said Bauer. Most projections say that tighter regulation, cleaner sources of electricity and higher-mileage vehicles will cut industrial emissions enough by the end of this century that farm emissions will be starved of the other ingredients necessary to create aerosols. A study this January showed that global industrial nitrogen oxide emissions declined from 2005 to 2014, even as farm emissions boomed. (Fast-growing China and India are exceptions.)

Production of artificial fertilizers has skyrocketed from about 20 million tons in 1950 to nearly 190 million tons today—about a third of them nitrogen-based. Fertilizer production will almost certainly keep growing to keep pace with human population, but the amount of aerosols created as a result depends on many factors, including air temperature, precipitation, season, time of day, wind patterns and of course the other needed ingredients from industrial or natural sources. (In parts of Africa, Asia and the Middle East, aerosols or their precursors come mainly from desert dust, sea spray or wildfires.) The largest increases in farm emissions will probably be in Africa, while the slowest projected growth rates are in Europe, says the study.

Fabien Paulot, an atmospheric chemist with Princeton University and the National Oceanic and Atmospheric Administration who was not involved in the study, said, "You might expect air quality would decline if ammonia emissions go up, but this shows it won't happen, provided the emissions from combustion go down." That means that pollutants other than ammonia should probably be targeted for abatement, he said.

Johannes Lelieveld, lead author of the 2015 *Nature* study disagreed. "The article underscores that all source categories should be controlled," he said. "One should be cautious about suggesting that food production could be increased" without increasing pollution, he said because that "critically depends" on the assumption that societies will successfully curb industrial emissions. Lelieveld cited the recent scandal over Volkswagen's fraudulent auto-emissions controls, and pointed out that even with the recent reductions in industrial pollution, most nations including the United States still have large areas that exceed the World Meteorological Organization's recommended maximum of 10 micrograms of fine particulates per cubic meter.

Bauer says that if future industrial emissions go down, much farm-produced ammonia will end up in earth's troposphere, roughly 2 to 10 kilometers from the surface. There, lightning and other natural processes may also help create fine particulates-"but it will be so high up, it won't be a problem for us," she said. Most of these particles would be trapped by raindrops and removed harmlessly, she says.

All this said, agricultural pollution raises other concerns. Vast quantities of excess fertilizers wash off fields each year, polluting huge watersheds; as just one example, each summer an oxygenless "dead zone" spreads from the mouth of the Mississippi River, fueled by excess nitrogen from upstream. More careful fertilizer application would solve a lot of this, said Bauer. On the other hand, industrial sulfates have been credited with reflecting solar radiation and thus slightly mitigating ongoing global warming caused by other fossil-fuel emissions. "It's all pollution, but in some sense, some of it is good," said Bauer. "We have to decide: Do we want a small cooling effect, or do we want clean air?"

Industrial Agriculture Dangerously Pollutes the Earth in Multiple Ways

The Food Empowerment Project

The Food Empowerment Project is an organization focused on creating sustainability through food choice. Among their platforms are the prevention of animal abuse, environmental pollution, unfair working conditions, and child labor.

In today's world there are a host of serious environmental problems, and factory farming is one of the top causes of pollution.[1] Scientific research has found that factory farming's method of crowding and confining animals in warehouse-like conditions before killing them and mass-producing both "meat" from cows, pigs and chickens as well as dairy and eggs poses "an unacceptable level of risk to public health and damage to the environment…"[2] Yet, despite factory farming's severe social and ecological costs, many governments promote this unsustainable industry to supply a growing global "meat" market that is projected to double by 2050.[3]

Factory Farm Pollutants

In general, there are two primary sources of factory farm pollution:

Waste from Animal Farms

Factory farms typically concentrate tens or hundreds of thousands of animals in one area, and a large operation can produce as much excrement as a small city.[4] According to the EPA, "A single dairy cow produces about 120 pounds of wet manure per day, which is equivalent to the waste produced by 20–40 people."[5] Using EPA statistics, that means California's 1.8 million dairy cows produce as much waste as 36–72 million people. So, when taking into

"Pollution (Water, Air, Chemicals)," Food Empowerment Project, foodispower.org. Reprinted by permission.

consideration tens or hundreds of thousands of animals, it's not surprising that this amounts to about 130 times more excrement than is produced by the entire human population every year.[6] For centuries, farmers have used animal manure to fertilize their fields, but factory farms produce far more waste than the land can absorb,[7] turning disposal of this toxic by-product into a big problem for both the agriculture industry and society.

Unlike human waste, animal excrement from factory farms is not processed as sewage, making it about 500 times more concentrated than treated human waste[8] while leaving pathogens and volatile chemicals intact.[9] Even so, farmers typically spray some liquidized manure onto the food being grown for animals using giant sprinkler jets, and store the rest in open-air cesspools that can be as large as several football fields[10] and hold millions of gallons of waste.[11] However, neither of these dispersal techniques is environmentally safe or sustainable.

Agricultural Chemicals

Past research has shown that of all the agricultural chemicals applied in the US, about 37 percent were used to grow crops for animals raised for food.[12] Agricultural chemicals (or agrichemicals) refer to the wide variety of chemical products used in agriculture, such as pesticides (including insecticides, herbicides and fungicides), as well as synthetic fertilizers, hormones and antibiotics. Farmers spray agricultural chemicals onto food grown for animals in order to kill bugs, rodents, weeds, and other organisms that would otherwise supplant or eat the grain grown for the animals. They also apply these substances directly to animals' skin, fur or feathers to combat insect infestation.[13]

However, many of the agricultural chemicals approved by the US Environmental Protection Agency (EPA) contain ingredients that are known carcinogens,[14] while others cause severe allergies, birth defects and various health problems.[15] In addition, those who grow food for animals rely heavily on synthetic petroleum-based fertilizers,[16] and animal waste itself contains residues from the massive doses of non-therapeutic antibiotics and artificial growth hormones that animals are routinely fed or injected with to prevent illness and accelerate weight gain.[17] Ultimately, the dangerous compounds found in agrichemicals end up as pollutants when wind and rain disperse them into the environment.

Environmental Impacts of Factory Farm Pollution

Factory farms dump tens of millions of tons of animal waste and agricultural chemicals into the environment every year—driving land, water and air pollution in the process:

Land Pollution

Most food produced for animals is grown using a combination of untreated animal waste and synthetic fertilizers, both of which contain excessive amounts of nitrogen, phosphorus and heavy metals (such as zinc, copper, chromium, arsenic, cadmium, and lead).[18] Even though most of these substances usually act as nutrients that nourish plants, industrial farmers overuse them to increase crop yields, and the remainder that cannot be absorbed into the earth—especially when it is already saturated after heavy rains[19]—ends up polluting the soil, while degrading its water retention ability and fertility over time.[20]

In addition, it's been shown that US farmers have actually used 750 million pounds of some 20,000 different agricultural chemicals in just one year,[21] and those that have been used to kill insects and weeds that threaten crop yields end up poisoning natural ecosystems. Plus, as some weeds and bugs have developed resistance to these compounds over the years, chemists have continued to create ever more powerfully-toxic pesticides that are even worse for the environment.

The residues of these chemicals are found at every level of the food chain, and—through the process of bioaccumulation—become more concentrated the higher up the chain one looks. Meaning, in a system that runs the gamut from micro-organisms to humans, people who eat animal products get the highest dosage of toxins.

Water Pollution

The National Water Quality Inventory report of 2002 noted that agricultural runoff was "the leading cause of river and stream impairment and the second leading cause of impairment in lakes, ponds and reservoirs,"[22] which includes fertilizer runoff that typically occurs when rain carries fertilizer into waterways. Runoff from both synthetic fertilizers and animal waste can poison drinking water and aquatic ecosystems, wreaking havoc on human health[23] and wildlife.[24] In the Southern US, where there is an abundance of chicken factory farms, as many as one-third of all underground wells fall below EPA safe drinking water standards for nitrate, a form of nitrogen concentrated in chicken waste.[25]

Excrement from animal waste cesspools can also seep through the soil into nearby groundwater and overflow during storms.[26] In 1995, for example, an eight-acre pig-manure lagoon in North Carolina ruptured, spilling 22 million gallons of untreated waste into the New River, which killed millions of fish.[27] In California, the nation's top dairy-producing state, a UC Davis study found animal agriculture to be responsible for serious nitrate contamination in areas with big dairy operations, and the authors of the study determined that nitrate would remain in those areas for decades even if all farming operations were eliminated.[28] According to the US Environmental Protection Agency, as of 2007, animal excrement from factory farms had contaminated groundwater in 17 states and polluted 35,000 miles of rivers in 22 states.[29]

Factory farm runoff also causes algal blooms that kill fish by depleting water of its oxygen, contributing to the formation of hundreds of "dead zones" worldwide where sea creatures cannot survive. The largest of these can be found in the Gulf of Mexico and is nearly the size of the State of New Jersey.[30]

Aquaculture (basically, the factory farming of fish in underwater enclosures) also makes a large contribution to water pollution, especially in the coastal mangrove swamps where these operations are typically located. Like land-based animal agriculture, intensive fish farming maximizes production efficiency by concentrating as many animals into the smallest amount of space possible—and also creates tons of untreated fecal waste that pollutes and de-oxygenates aquatic habitats.

Air Pollution

Various gases from animal waste are all major sources of factory farm air pollution,[31] and particulate matter and bacterial toxins found in high concentrations at and around industrialized animal facilities have caused serious respiratory[32] and cardiac disorders.[33] The ammonia from waste slurry lagoons also breeds bacteria, which creates acid that evaporates and combines with nitrous oxide from fertilizers and industrial pollution to form nitric acid rain—which leaches nutrients from the soil, despoils forest habitats, and kills fish by releasing toxic minerals from the earth that flow into aquatic ecosystems. Even though agricultural fertilizer emissions are the leading cause of nitric acid rain (after motor vehicles and coal plants), they remain virtually unregulated in the US.[34]

In addition, animal agriculture is responsible for more than half of humanity's total greenhouse gas emissions[35] (largely created by using arable land to grow food for animals, animal belching and flatulence, and chemical emanations from manure). This includes 37 percent of anthropogenic (i.e., human-made) methane, and methane gas is 23 times more potent a climate change agent than carbon dioxide.[36] Yet, despite factory farming's leading role in the climate change crisis, the EPA does not currently have the authority to regulate the US livestock industry's greenhouse gas emissions.[37]

How You Can Help

Taking a stand against factory farming's ecological destructiveness by becoming vegan is not only better for your health, but also saves the lives of animals. You can take environmental eating a step further by supporting organic farmers who don't use agricultural chemicals and synthetic fertilizers. Eating organic can also improve your health—and helps reduce the number of farm workers exposed to toxic chemicals too.

References

1. "Livestock's Long Shadow: Environmental Issues and Options," The United Nations: Food and Agriculture Organization, 2006. Retrieved 3/5/2013 from http://www.fao.org/docrep/010/a0701e/a0701e00.HTM.

2. "Putting Meat on the Table: Industrial Farm Animal Production in America," Pew Commission on Industrial Farm Animal Production, 2008. http://www.ncifap.org /bin/e/j/PCIFAPFin.pdf (11/13/10).

3. Bittman, Mark. "Rethinking the Meat Guzzler," *The New York Times*, 2008. http:// www.nytimes.com/2008/01/27/weekinreview/27bittman.html (11/13/10).

4. "Facts About Pollution from Livestock Farms," National Resources Defense Council, 2005. http://www.nrdc.org/water/pollution/ffarms.asp (11/13/10).

5. "Notes from Underground," US Environmental Protection Agency, Fall 2001. (8/05/17) http://bit.ly/2zv18Ft.

6. Moore, Heather. "You Can't Be a Meat-Eating Environmentalist," *American Chronicle*, 2007. http://www.americanchronicle.com/articles/view/24825 (11/13/10).

7. "Putting Meat on the Table: Industrial Farm Animal Production in America," Pew Commission on Industrial Farm Animal Production, 2008. http://www.ncifap.org /bin/e/j/PCIFAPFin.pdf (11/13/10).

8. "Putting Meat on the Table: Industrial Farm Animal Production in America," Pew Commission on Industrial Farm Animal Production, 2008. http://www.ncifap.org /bin/e/j/PCIFAPFin.pdf (11/13/10).

9. Wiley, K., Vucinich, N., Miller, J., & Vanzi, M. (2004, November). "Confined Animal Facilities in California." http://sor.senate.ca.gov/sites/sor.senate.ca.gov /files/%7BD51D1D55-1B1F-4268-80CC-C636EE939A06%7D.pdf (08/05/17).

10. "Report Documents Waste Lagoons' Threats to Environment, Public Health," Natural Resources Defense Council, 2001. http://www.laondaverde.org/media /pressReleases/010724.asp (08/15/17).

11. "Hurricane Matthew Killed Millions of Farm Animals in North Carolina," *Mother Jones*, 2016. http://bit.ly/2hXq3aP (10/20/17).

12. "Livestock's Long Shadow: Environmental Issues and Options," The United Nations: Food and Agriculture Organization, 2006. http://www.fao.org/docrep /010/a0701e/a0701e00.htm (11/13/10).

13. "Agricultural Chemical Usage Swine and Swine Facilities." US Department of Agriculture, National Agricultural Statistics Service, 2006. http://usda.mannlib

.cornell.edu/usda/current/AgChemUseSwine/AgChemUseSwine-12-20-2006.txt
(11/13/10).

14. "Reducing Environmental Cancer Risk: What We Can Do Now," The President's
Cancer Panel, 2010. https://deainfo.nci.nih.gov/advisory/pcp/annualreports
/pcp08-09rpt/pcp_report_08-09_508.pdf.

15. "Potential Health Effects of Pesticides," (November 6, 2017). Retrieved November
09, 2017 from https://extension.psu.edu/potential-health-effects-of-pesticides-2.

16. Horrigan, L., Lawrence, R., Walker, P. "How Sustainable Agriculture Can
Address the Environmental and Human Health Harms of Industrial Agriculture,"
Center for a Livable Future, Johns Hopkins Bloomberg School of Public Health,
Environmental Health Perspectives, 2002. https://www.ncbi.nlm.nih.gov/pmc
/articles/PMC1240832/pdf/ehp0110-000445.pdf (4/12/13).

17. Orlando, E., Kolok, A., et al. "Endocrine-Disrupting Effects of Cattle Feedlot
Effluent on an Aquatic Sentinel Species, the Fathead Minnow," Environmental
Health Perspectives, Vol. 112(3), p. 346–52; March 2004. Retrieved 3/7/2013 from
http://www.ncbi.nlm.nih.gov/pmc/articles/PMC1241866/pdf/ehp0112-000353
.pdf.

18. Li, Y., McCrory, F., et al. "A Survey of Selected Heavy Metal Concentrations in
Wisconsin Dairy Feeds," American Dairy Science Association, 2005. http://
download.journals.elsevierhealth.com/pdfs/journals/0022-0302/
PIIS0022030205729726.pdf (11/13/10).

19. Hamilton, Keegan, "Craptastrophe: Record Rainfall Has Created a Dung
Dilemma for Missouri Farmers," The River Front Times, July 9, 2008. http://
www.riverfronttimes.com/2008-07-09/news/craptastrophe-record-rainfall-has
-created-a-dung-dilemma-for-missouri-farmers/ (11/23/10).

20. Horrigan, L., Lawrence, R., Walker, P. "How Sustainable Agriculture Can Address
the Environmental and Human Health Harms of Industrial Agriculture,"
Center for a Livable Future, Johns Hopkins Bloomberg School of Public Health,
Environmental Health Perspectives, 2002. https://www.ncbi.nlm.nih.gov/pmc
/articles/PMC1240832/pdf/ehp0110-000445.pdf (4/12/13).

21. Fano, Alix, Lethal Laws, 1997, page 108.

22. "Water Contamination," Centers for Disease Control and Contamination,
2016. https://www.cdc.gov/healthywater/other/agricultural/contamination.html
(10/20/17).

23. Moore, Heather. "Tyson Fined $2M For Mucking Up Missouri River," Care2.org,
2009. http://www.care2.com/causes/environment/blog/tyson-fined-2m-for
-mucking-up-missouri-river/ (11/13/10).

24. Royte, Elizabeth. "Transsexual Frogs: A Popular Weed Killer Makes Some Frogs
Grow the Wrong Sex Organs. Your Drinking Water May Have 30 Times the Dose
They're Getting," Discover, February 2003. http://discovermagazine.com/2003/feb
/featfrogs (11/13/10).

25. Goodman, Peter S. "An Unsavory Byproduct," *Washington Post*, August 1, 1999. http://www.washingtonpost.com/wp-srv/local/daily/aug99/chicken1.htm (11/23/10).

26. Moore, Heather. "Tyson Fined $2M For Mucking Up Missouri River." Care2.org, 2009. http://www.care2.com/causes/environment/blog/tyson-fined-2m-for -mucking-up-missouri-river/ (11/13/10).

27. "CAFOs and Environmental Justice: The Case of North Carolina," *Environmental Health Perspectives*, 2013. https://ehp.niehs.nih.gov/121-a182/ (10/20/17).

28. "Groundwater Nitrate Contamination Grows in California Farm Areas," *Los Angeles Times*, 2012. http://articles.latimes.com/2012/mar/14/local/la-me-water -nitrate-20120314 (10/20/17).

29. Weeks, Jennifer. "Factory Farms," *CQ Researcher*, January 12, 2007. https:// prairierivers.org/wp-content/uploads/2009/12/factory-farms.pdf (11/13/10).

30. Roach, John. "Gulf of Mexico 'Dead Zone' Is Size of New Jersey," *National Geographic News*. May 25, 2005. http://news.nationalgeographic.com/news /2005/05/0525_050525_deadzone.html (11/13/10).

31. "Manure Gas Dangers Fact Sheet." Farm Safety Association, 2002. http:// www.sustainabletable.org/issues/airpollution/footnotes/7_8_18.pdf (11/13/10).

32. "Controlling Livestock Ammonia Emissions Could Reduce Harmful Atmospheric Particulates Blanketing US East Coast," *ScienceDaily*, March 9, 2007. http:// www.sciencedaily.com/releases/2007/02/070227105447.htm (11/23/2010).

33. Brigham, K., and Meyrick, D. "Endotoxin and Lung Injury." *American Review of Respiratory Disease*, May 1986. http://www.ncbi.nlm.nih.gov/ pubmed/3085564?dopt=Citation (11/13/10).

34. Tennesen, Michael. "Sour Showers: Acid Rain Returns—This Time It Is Caused by Nitrogen Emissions," *Scientific American*, June 21, 2010. http:// www.scientificamerican.com/article.cfm?id=acid-rain-caused-by-nitrogen -emissions (11/26/10).

35. Goodland, R., and Anhang, J. "Livestock and Climate Change," World Watch Institute, 2009. http://www.worldwatch.org/files/pdf/Livestock%20and%20 Climate%20Change.pdf (11/13/10).

36. "Livestock's Long Shadow: Environmental Issues and Options," The United Nations: Food and Agriculture Organization, 2006. http://www.fao.org /docrep/010/a0701e/a0701e00.htm (03/07/13).

37. Bravender, R., Geman, B., et al. "Farm Interests Use EPA Spending Bill to Fight Climate Regs," *The New York Times*, 2009. http://www.nytimes.com/gwire /2009/06/19/19greenwire-farm-interests-use-epa-spending-bill-to-fight-85048 .html (11/13/10).

Industrial Agriculture Mandates Deforestation

The Food and Agriculture Organization of the
United Nations

The Food and Agriculture Organization of the United Nations (FAO)
is at the forefront of international efforts to defeat hunger. They work
in over 130 countries around the world.

It is not necessary to cut down forests in order to produce more food, says *The State of the World's Forests 2016* report.

In Latin America, commercial agriculture is the main cause of deforestation, according to a new FAO report, *The State of the World's Forests 2016* (*SOFO*).

SOFO notes that commercial agriculture generated almost 70% of deforestation in Latin America between 2000–2010, but only one third in Africa, where small-scale farming is a more significant factor in deforestation.

In the Amazon in particular agribusiness production for international markets was the main factor behind deforestation since 1990, as a result of practices such as extensive grazing, cultivation of soy and palm oil plantations.

"Commercial agriculture in the region cannot continue to grow at the expense of the region's forests and natural resources," said Jorge Meza, Senior FAO Forestry Officer.

Meza—who heads FAO's regional initiative for sustainable use of natural resources—emphasized that policies such as linking agricultural incentives with environmental criteria, the adoption of silvopastoral practices, payment for environmental services and the recovery of degraded pastures can prevent the expansion of the agricultural frontier at the expense of forests.

Food and Agriculture Organization of the United Nations, July 18, 2016, "FAO: Commercial Agriculture Accounted for Almost 70 Percent of Deforestation in Latin America," http://www.fao.org/americas/noticias/ver/en/c/425600/. Reproduced with permission.

"Hunger eradication and food security can be reached through agricultural intensification and measures such as social protection, rather than through expansion of agricultural areas at the expense of forests," Meza said.

While deforestation remains high in the region, in 2015 the rate of deforestation has been reduced by almost 50% compared to 1990. This reduction has also been significant in the Amazon, the product of sustainable development policies driven by countries sharing the Amazon basin.

According to *SOFO*, over 20 countries succeeded in improving food security while maintaining or increasing forest cover since 1990, demonstrating that it is not necessary to cut down forests in order to produce more food.

Expansion of Pastures: Main Cause of Deforestation

A study cited by the *SOFO* on the causes of deforestation in seven countries in South America showed the relationship between deforestation and the expansion of extensive grazing.

According to the study, between 1990–2005, 71% of deforestation in Argentina, Colombia, Bolivia, Brazil, Paraguay, Peru and Venezuela was due to increased demand for pasture; 14% due to cash crops; and less than 2% to infrastructure and urban sprawl.

The expansion of pastures caused the loss of at least one third of the forests in six of the countries analysed. The exception was Peru, where the increase of small scale farming was the dominant factor driving deforestation, causing 41% of the total.

In Argentina, the expansion of pastures was responsible for 45% of deforestation, while the expansion of commercial agriculture accounted for more than 43%. In Brazil, more than 80% of deforestation was associated with forests being cut down for pasture.

Linking Agricultural Subsidies to Environmental Standards

In several countries, agricultural subsidies have encouraged large-scale deforestation as they increase the profitability of agricultural production and generate pressure to expand the agricultural frontier. Examples in the region are extensive grazing and soybean production on an industrial scale.

One policy option to avoid this is to link the incentives and public funds that commercial agriculture receives to environmental standards and norms.

SOFO notes that a single reform of this kind in Brazil, which linked subsidies to rural credit with environmental criteria, prevented the loss of 270 thousand hectares of forests that would have been deforested to increase beef production.

The *"Bolsa Verde"* Brazilian initiative is another example: a conditional cash transfer program that delivers resources to thousands of poor families in exchange for keeping vegetation cover and sustainably managing their natural resources.

Costa Rica: The Value of Environmental Services

According to *SOFO*, after deforestation reached its peak in Costa Rica in the 1980s, today forests cover 54% of its surface, thanks to structural changes in the economy and the priority given to the conservation and sustainable management of forests.

Incentives for forest plantations were replaced in the mid-1990s by the Payment for Environmental Services, PES. This program has been used to strengthen the system of protected areas and create biological corridors covering 437,000 hectares.

The program offered incentives to farmers who planted 5.4 million trees, in addition to supporting forest conservation in indigenous territories.

In total, between 1996 and 2015, investments in PES projects related to forests in Costa Rica reached 318 million USD; 64% of these funds came from taxes on fossil fuels and 22% from World Bank loans.

"These initiatives have also been developed by other countries in the region, such as Ecuador's SocioForest Program and forestry development policies in Guatemala" Meza said.

The Role of Plantations and the Private Sector

One way to reduce pressure on native forests is the development of forest plantations.

In Uruguay, for example, the forest plantation area increased by about 40 thousand hectares per year in the period 2008–2011, with an estimated annual investment of $48 million.

In Chile, since 1990, more than 1 million hectares of plantations have been created. From 2025, these plantations should sustainably produce about 50 million cubic meters of wood per year.

According to *SOFO*, plantations in Chile have reduced pressure on natural forests, where industrial logging was reduced from 16.1% of total logging in 1990 to 0.8% in 2013.

Since 1990 there has been an increase of 8% of the area of primary forest and other naturally regenerated forests in Chile. However, the *SOFO* warns that in some cases plantations have replaced natural forests.

Agribusiness Can Promote and Adhere to Sustainable Agriculture Practices

Natasha Geiling

Natasha Geiling is an environmental journalist whose work has been published by ThinkProgress, Smithsonian Magazine, *and* Atlas Obscura. *She is currently a student at Berkeley Law School.*

On Tuesday, one of the world's largest traders of agricultural commodities vowed to help curb forest loss by instating a "No-Deforestation" policy for soy and palm oil in its supply chain.

Archer Daniels Midland's no-deforestation policy will be the first of its kind to cover soy production outside of the Brazilian Amazon. It also comes at a crucial time for the Amazon rainforest, which is especially affected by soy production and has seen a recent uptick agriculturally-driven deforestation. As of 2012, soybean production had caused the loss of 80 million hectares of forests in the Amazon basin.

Under the new policy, Archer Daniels Midland—known as ADM—will work with the Forest Trust, a non-profit group dedicated to improving the sustainability of company supply chains. The groups will work to map ADM's supply chain, making sure that none of its soy or palm oil products come from areas where ecosystems are threatened. The company will formally announce the plan, along with more details, on May 7, [2015].

Deforestation is a leading driver of climate change. According to *Scientific American*, loss of tropical rainforests releases more carbon dioxide into the atmosphere than the sum total of all cars. Though tropical deforestation is primarily caused by expanding agriculture, ADM's announcement is just the most recent in a string of commitments by food and agriculture companies to begin ending tropical deforestation.

"Agribusiness Giant Adopts Historic No-Deforestation Policy," by Natasha Geiling, *ThinkProgress*, April 1, 2015. Reprinted by permission.

"ADM has a steadfast commitment to the development of traceable and transparent agricultural supply chains that protect forests worldwide," the company's chief communications officer Victoria Podesta said in an emailed statement. "We are confident that our No Deforestation policy is both strong and appropriate for our company. It combines a clear commitment to no deforestation with progressive action focused on our most critical supply chains."

ADM, based in Chicago but with a market reach that spans six continents, buys all of its soy and palm oil from third parties. And while the palm oil industry has seen remarkable improvement in its deforestation policies—with nearly 96 percent of the market controlled by no-deforestation commitments—the soy industry has lagged behind in adopting similar policies, making ADM's commitment to ending deforestation in the soy supply chain the first of its kind.

"While there's still a lot of work to be done to implement these palm oil policies on the ground and to reign in rogue actors, we're really looking to now spread this transformation to other commodities that drive deforestation in other parts of the world—soy in Latin America being top among them," Ben Cushing, a spokesman for the advocacy group Forest Heroes, told *ThinkProgress*.

Over the last decade, Brazil appeared to be making huge strides in curbing deforestation in the Amazon, thanks in large part to pressure exerted by activists on soy and cattle farmers. Instead of cutting down forests to make way for farmland and grazing areas, farmers started to think of ways to make existing farmland more productive. It seemed to be working, with deforestation in Brazil dropping 70 percent between 2005 and 2014.

Part of the slow in deforestation also came in 2006 when major soybean traders—ADM among them—agreed to not buy soy grown on deforested Amazon land in Brazil. Known as the Soy Moratorium, the agreement really did help slow the pace of deforestation in Brazil's Amazon.

But signs suggest that the pause in deforestation is over—and that loss of the Amazon rainforest is spreading beyond Brazil to peripheral countries like Peru and Bolivia, where the Soy Moratorium doesn't exist. The moratorium also fails to protect other areas of Brazil, like the Cerrado, a vast tropical savanna whose waters feed crucial river basins like the Amazon. And as the world's growing economy increases the demand for meat, the demand for soy will also increase, because 75 percent of the world's soy is used as animal feed.

"We're at a critical juncture now to break the link between agriculture, especially for soy production and deforestation in Latin America," Cushing said. "The recent progress on palm oil shows that this is possible, and now ADM's announcement is a major step forward for the soy industry."

Investor advocacy played a crucial role in encouraging ADM to commit to the policy, with Green Century Capital Management, an environmentally responsible investment company, teaming up with the New York State Pension Fund file a shareholder proposal that raised concerns about deforestation in the company's supply chain. The New York State Pension Fund, which is the third largest pension fund in the nation, currently holds around 1,795,201 shares of ADM worth around $83.1 million.

"Shareholders are essentially the only stakeholder that corporations are required to respond to," Lucia von Reusner, Green Century's shareholder advocate, told *ThinkProgress*. "As a shareholder we have a unique voice at the board level that other stakeholders don't have."

In the past year, Green Century also encouraged Kellogg's, Smuckers, and ConAgra to commit to purchasing palm oil from sources that don't contribute to deforestation.

Now, they've set their sights on influencing the world's largest distributors. At the same time that Green Century filed a shareholder proposal with ADM, they filed a similar proposal with Bunge, a direct competitor. So far, von Reusner said Bunge has not responded to the proposal, but she expects that it will head to a board vote near the end of May.

"The fact that ADM has made this commitment has such huge influence over the global agriculture supply chain and global food production," von Reusner said, noting that it's difficult for farmers to prioritize long-term sustainability over short-term cost cutting unless large companies use their influence to demand it. "It's important that these companies that are setting the market are saying that, in addition to a low price, it's important that our suppliers adhere to sustainable practices."

Consumer Actions Result in Agribusiness Turning to Sustainable Practices

Olivia Boyd

Olivia Boyd writes for the Guardian *and reports on sustainable business.*

When John Sauven, executive director at Greenpeace UK, heard a woman complain on the radio that supermarket croissants were cheaper to buy wrapped in plastic than paper, he was so startled he went straight to his local Co-op.

"It was true," Sauven said at a recent *Guardian* roundtable discussion on the future of waste. "If I bought two croissants in a brown paper bag, it was 79p [each], and if I bought them in a big plastic container it was 63p [each]. And I just thought … this is a complete failure of the system."

The failure, of course, goes far beyond croissants. From the 300,000 tonnes of clothing the UK sent to landfill last year to the 7m coffee cups we chuck out each day, the scale of our throwaway habits are startlingly clear.

So too are the impacts: images of bags and bottles washed up on beaches, or sea life tangled in plastic netting, give grim credence to the Ellen MacArthur Foundation's now familiar prediction that the oceans will contain more plastic than fish by 2050.

The role of business in addressing this crisis has become the subject of fierce debate in industry and policy circles. And that was clearly on show at a *Guardian* roundtable event, sponsored by recycling and resource management company Suez.

New Business Models Needed

A key idea under discussion was the circular economy, a model that aims to keep resources in a perpetual, benign cycle, rather than send them to the dump after first use. While companies at the table, including Marks & Spencer and the Co-op, have publicly embraced the concept, Sauven argued that without greater ambition and more radical change from business, the circular economy risked becoming another buzzword.

"We need to make sure this doesn't just replace sustainability … and that we keep creating words which don't actually mean very much in terms of substance," Sauven said. "What we're talking about is not just tinkering with the system, we're talking about a much more systemic shift."

A particular flashpoint for the roundtable was the release of a new packaging plan by Coca-Cola. The soft drinks giant has become emblematic of big business's contribution to the waste problem thanks in part to a high profile campaign by Greenpeace, which claims the company generates more than 100bn plastic bottles a year.

Coca-Cola has promised to up the recycled content of its bottles to 50% by 2020 and research the impact of deposit return schemes (DRS), where consumers are asked to pay a refundable deposit on cans or bottles. It has also launched a campaign "to encourage people to recycle and dissuade littering," said Nick Brown, head of sustainability at Coca-Cola European Partners.

"We know communication on recycling is really difficult, it tends to be quite factual … there's a bit more we think can be done to change behaviour, around making more of an emotional connection and explaining the benefits of recycling."

For Carina Millstone, executive director at food waste campaign group Feedback, these pledges missed the true scope of the change needed to create a sustainable society. In fact, she argued, the resource-extractive, consumption-based business model of a global corporation such as Coca-Cola was fundamentally incompatible with the needs of the planet.

"The idea of driving public awareness, making it easier for people [to recycle], isn't going to cut it … Coca-Cola will not exist if we achieve sustainability. That's the reality of it," she said.

New business models that promote longevity and durability of goods are needed instead, argued Millstone. Such a transformation would require a "re-regionalisation of economies," away from the low-cost globalised production model that has made it cheaper, for example, to buy a new pair of shoes than repair old ones, she said.

"Back in the day, we had cobblers all over the place. We don't any more … because the big companies that dominate and create our way of life have figured out it's cheaper to manufacture shoes elsewhere, taking advantage of lax environmental regulation and poor resource use, and the relative cost of labour."

Local Creativity

Millstone is not alone in seeing a "local, vibrant economy" as key to solving an integrated set of resource and social challenges. Already, the UK is dotted with repair cafes, which provide tools, materials and advice to locals wanting to fix anything from bicycles to crockery.

Sophie Unwin, founder of Remade in Edinburgh, a social enterprise that teaches repair skills and sells refurbished computers and furniture, is part of this movement. As well as keeping goods out of landfill, her business has created 10 jobs over the past three years, she said.

Meanwhile, Cat Fletcher, the Brighton-based director of online reuse network Freegle, has been working with artists and designers to turn hard-to-recycle goods such as office in-trays into new items like sunglasses and light fittings.

"There's a great opportunity with hyper-local creativity," said Fletcher. "It's happening all over the world. There's Precious Plastics who are making little machines, which you can literally have at home and reprocess your own plastic, and maybe turn it into fibre for a 3D printer, or mould it into pot plants.

"There's an entire mall in Sweden which only has second-hand, upcycled goods … There is unlimited potential in what you can do. It's a matter of tapping into the existing people and helping them."

Calls for Government Action

But can this community approach drive change fast enough? David Palmer-Jones, chief executive of Suez UK, which processes around 9m tonnes of waste per year, was doubtful. "What we fail to recognise is the scale," he said. "Local initiatives are fantastic to show what can be done ... [But] to get scale and get speed of change we require government intervention."

While there were calls for the government to implement a compulsory, nationwide DRS, Iain Ferguson, environment manager at the Co-op, warned against clumsy, top-down solutions.

"Voluntary systems give you the opportunity to be flexible and innovative," he said. "Badly designed mandatory schemes shut that down." The correct approach would fuse the two and incorporate a system of rewards, he added.

For many around the table, better coordination at Westminster, where responsibility for waste falls between different departments, was essential. Phil Cumming, senior sustainability manager at M&S, pointed to Scotland—which has a dedicated agency, Zero Waste Scotland, to deliver the government's circular economy strategy—as a more effective example.

Rauno Raal, chief executive of the organisation that runs Estonia's hugely successful DRS, argued that his country also offered a useful lesson. Since 2005, Estonian customers have paid shops a deposit on a bottle of cola, for example, which they can reclaim as a discount on the next purchase if they return the empty bottle. Last year, 75% of cans and 87% of PET bottles were returned.

The scheme was only made possible, said Raal, by government action. "The discussion here is exactly the same as in Estonia 12 years ago. All the retailers were afraid, the producers were afraid ... everyone was fighting against the return scheme. The government asked all the producers and retailers to be at the table and said, very clearly, 'OK, you don't want a DRS, then we will do it as a governmental institution.'"

But if the government is key, so too are citizens, added Raal, saying that personal values—inculcated by family and teachers—were vital to changing consumption patterns and conserving resources.

Adam Lusby, lecturer in circular economy implementation at the University of Exeter, disagreed. Consumers—and consumption—were the wrong target, he said. "We don't need to go on a big campaign to change people's behaviour, we just need to change how we design stuff."

That means better product design, but also a better designed economy, one which, as a first step, would tax non-renewable resources, such as the fossil fuels used to make plastic, rather than labour: "Instead of fighting over who does what, there are some good, healthy, macro economic decisions that can be made," Lusby said.

Roundtable Attendees

- **Oliver Balch (chair),** journalist and author
- **Jane Bevis,** chair, OPRL
- **Piotr Barczak**, policy officer on waste, European Environmental Bureau
- **Nick Brown**, head of sustainability, Coca-Cola European Partners
- **Phil Cumming**, senior sustainability manager, Marks & Spencer
- **Iain Ferguson**, environment manager, the Co-op
- **Cat Fletcher**, co-founder and media director, Freegle
- **Adam Lusby**, lecturer in circular economy implementation, University of Exeter
- **Carina Millstone**, executive director, Feedback
- **David Palmer-Jones**, CEO, Suez recycling and recovery UK
- **Rauno Raal**, CEO, Pandipakend (Estonia)
- **John Sauven**, UK executive director, Greenpeace
- **Sophie Unwin**, director, The Edinburgh Remakery
- **Ugo Vallauri**, business development lead and co-founder, Re-start

Industrial Agriculture Is More Effective at Environmental Conservation than Small Farms

Ted Nordhaus

Ted Nordhaus is the Founder and Executive Director of the Breakthrough Institute, a global research center that identifies and promotes technological solutions to environmental and human development challenges.

The following keynote address was delivered by Ted Nordhaus at the first annual Institute for Food and Agricultural Literacy Symposium on June 3, 2015. The speech has been lightly edited.

Thank you for having me today. It has come to my attention during the course of this conference that the fast food chain Chipotle has announced that it will no longer serve food grown with genetically modified organisms. Apparently, this occurred last month, but somehow I missed it on Twitter. Between the debut of Caitlyn Jenner, the latest royal baby, and the FIFA corruption scandal, I guess it just slipped through my stream.

I'm kidding, of course. If you follow food politics on social media or pretty much anywhere else, I dare say it would be impossible not to know that Chipotle has decided to phase out GMOs. In this way, what you think about GMOs has become a proxy for what you think about food and agriculture more broadly. GMO opponents are actually quite clear about this. What they are really after, many will tell you, is the "food system" itself—globalization, Monsanto, corporate agriculture, pesticides, synthetic fertilizer, monoculture, and the rest.

GMO advocates have been less clear about this. Outside the corridors of Monsanto and Archer Daniels Midland, there hasn't been a lot of stomach for defending industrial agriculture. As I

"The Environmental Case for Industrial Agriculture," by Ted Nordhaus, The Breakthrough Institute, June 8, 2015. Reprinted by permission.

will argue to you today, this is a problem. For at the bottom of contemporary debates about food and agriculture lay a series of fundamental misconceptions about agriculture that have become an obstacle to improving our food system.

Agriculture involves harvesting some portion of the earth's primary productivity, the processes though which energy is converted into organic material via photosynthesis in order to sustain us. Early human populations began to find ways to do this more efficiently and at greater scales long before the invention of agriculture, mostly by burning forests to create open meadows and grasslands that were better for hunting and supported larger mammal populations and hence more protein on each hectare of land.

The subsequent development of agriculture represented not a break, but rather an intensification of this process. Gradually, humans began to domesticate the grasses and mammals that pre-agricultural hunting and foraging were already selecting. With domestication, these processes simply accelerated. Humans systematically raised yields and intensified agricultural systems by selecting seeds and irrigating, developing ploughs to turn the soil, and domesticating livestock to work and fertilize the land. As a result, agricultural yields rose dramatically over centuries and millennia.

Broadly speaking, the long-term intensification of agriculture was driven by two heavily intertwined processes: first, increasing inputs of labor, capitol, and resources to increase the productivity of the land; and second, improving routines and technologies to direct that productivity toward outputs that humans desire—in other words, excluding unwanted plants, animals, and insects from the sites of agricultural production.

This is not ancient history. These trends and processes continue today. On a planet of seven-going-on-nine billion people, agricultural systems that do not both increase the productivity of land under cultivation and capture as much of that productivity for human consumption as possible will be neither practical nor sustainable. As such, arguments about agriculture and food that ignore these two imperatives are at best incoherent and at worst pernicious.

Let me use two contemporary controversies to illustrate this: the butterfly and the bee.

Monarch butterfly populations have declined significantly in recent years and many people have pointed the finger at two culprits, GMO corn and the herbicide glyphosate, otherwise known as Roundup. The former association is simply specious, but the latter is not. There is a correlation between glyphosate use and butterfly decline. But it's not that glyphosate is killing the butterfly. It is an herbicide that targets plants, not insects. Rather, glyphosate is killing milkweed, a weed in which monarchs lay their eggs. While the decline of monarch butterflies is an unintended consequence of glyphosate use, the elimination of milkweed is not. It is one of the weeds that the herbicide is supposed to get rid of.

The trade-off here is straightforward and zero sum. You can either have more milkweed in cornfields or higher yields, but you can't have both. If you choose more milkweed, then you are choosing lower yields, and, all else being equal, that means putting more land under cultivation to achieve the same level of agricultural output. With that comes attendant losses of habitat and biodiversity elsewhere.

Ultimately, the only way to have more monarch butterflies without reducing agricultural output or saving monarchs at the expense of other species is to create more monarch habitat outside of cornfields. This is an effort that a lot of people more concerned about monarch preservation as opposed to scoring ideological points about the food system have begun to focus on.

Like monarch butterflies, honeybees have also become a cause célèbre in the ongoing food debates. In recent years, beekeepers have been losing significantly higher percentages of their bees and hives to various ailments, with many advocates pointing the finger at a particular class of insecticide know as neonicotinoids. In the name of honeybees, the European Union has banned neonicotinoids, and the US Environmental Protection Agency, under pressure from environmental groups, is considering following suit.

In reality, there is scant evidence that these pesticides are a major contributor to bee deaths. The studies that do purport to show a direct link have been poorly designed and widely rejected by entomologists. And while Europe, which has banned neonicotinoids, continues to experience heavy bee losses, Australia, which hasn't banned them, has not.

Notwithstanding the cause of rising bee mortality, perhaps what is most interesting is that, despite rising losses, bee populations have not declined at all. The vast majority of bees live neither in the wild nor in backyard hives but are kept by industrial beekeepers, many of whom keep tens of thousands of hives that they ship around the country on semi-trucks to provide pollination services year-round.

Die-offs have always been a fact of life for beekeepers and are likely to remain so. But bee populations have remained stable because we have become expert at breeding queens and splitting hives. With or without neonicotinoids, that basic system of pollinating crops will almost certainly continue, as relying upon wild pollination and small-scale beekeeping could not possibly meet the pollination demands of American agriculture.

As I noted at the beginning, at bottom of both these controversies are fundamental misunderstandings of what agriculture is. Commercial honeybees are hardly more natural these days than the pesticides that activists claim are killing them, and every bit as much an agricultural technology. Monarch butterflies are increasingly unable to thrive in cornfields because we dedicate that land to the production of corn, not butterflies. Both cases are not novel expressions of an industrial food system gone haywire but rather reflect what the food system is, and has always been. Both domesticated honeybees and herbicides are used to increase the productivity of the land and to monopolize the outputs for human purposes.

Failure to understanding these basic dynamics too often results in advocacy and policy that is simply misguided. In the name of maintaining bee populations that are not at any particular risk from neonicotinoids, the EU and now the EPA are proposing banning the pesticides, which in all likelihood will be replaced by organophosphate pesticides that are vastly more toxic to wildlife of all kinds. Making it harder to keep milkweed out of cornfields and hence maintain higher yields will almost certainly result in putting more land under cultivation somewhere else, with impacts for habitat and biodiversity that might be significantly worse.

Debates about specific agricultural technologies and environmental impacts often lose sight of the forest through the trees in terms of the relationship between food production and the environment. Low-productivity food systems have devastating impacts on the environment. As much as three-quarters of all deforestation globally occurred prior to the Industrial Revolution, almost entirely due to two related uses, clearing land for agriculture and using wood for energy. Indeed, many places that we now think of as vast wilderness were once farmed. Even the Amazon basin, long thought to have been a primeval Eden turns out to have been the site of extensive agriculture prior to the decimation of the pre-Columbian population due to conquest and disease. Today, forests have come back in New England and many other parts of the world not due to disease, privation, or genocide but rather because agricultural productivity has risen so dramatically that many marginal agricultural lands have been abandoned.

Meanwhile, everywhere that people depend upon bushmeat for protein, forests and other habitat continue to be defaunated. Moreover, low-intensity pasturing of livestock represents the largest single human land use, larger even than cropland. When leading public intellectuals and chefs like Michael Pollan and Alice Waters decry feedlot meat and rhapsodize about the culinary and environmental benefits of grass-fed beef, what they are really proposing is a vast expansion of human impacts on the land.

Even with much lower levels of per-capita beef consumption, there is no way that American beef consumption, much less global consumption, could be met with pastured beef without dedicating much more land to pasture. Even accounting for the immense amount of grain needed to feed cattle, feedlot beef is more land efficient than grass-fed.

In short, were such a thing even possible, attempting to feed a world of seven-going-on-nine billion people with a preindustrial food system would almost certainly result in a massive expansion of human impacts through accelerated conversion of forests, grasslands, and other habitat to cropland and pasture.

It is perhaps no surprise that these kinds of errors would take hold in a society in which so few of us actually work in the agricultural sector. The archetypal farm in the public imagination is roughly the farm that existed around the turn of the last century, when most people in the United States left farming.

At that time, roughly half of the US population worked in agriculture. A century earlier, that number was closer to 90%. Without modern agriculture you cannot have modern life. There are literally no examples where societies have achieved modern living standards—universal education, healthcare, electrification, and so on—without moving most of the population off the land and out of agriculture. Without modern agriculture, most of us could not live in cities, go to college, or have professional careers. A world in which celebrity chefs can open farm-to-table restaurants and cultural creatives can patronize them is, ironically, only possible after industrial agriculture has liberated most of us from farming.

To be clear, modern agriculture is characterized by no shortage of charnel horrors—labor exploitation, factory farms, and poisoned land. I make these observations about the nature of agriculture and the modern food system not to absolve industrial agriculture of its problems, but rather to offer some more useful parameters for thinking about what we should want from our food system. In that spirit, let me suggest a few basic principles.

First, and most importantly, the food system globally needs to grow enough food to meet the basic nutritional needs of somewhere in the vicinity of nine billion people by the middle of this century. While the discussion in recent years about food and nutrition in the United States has been heavily focused on obesity, the reality is that much of the world still needs to consume more calories, not less. Nearly a billion people globally still struggle to meet their basic, daily caloric needs. Several billions more are just beginning to consume modest levels of dietary protein and fat. Suffice to say that the daily ration of farm-fresh vegetables that for so many of us symbolizes a healthful diet is still beyond the means of most people on the planet.

Second, the food system needs to liberate most of the global population from work on the farm and all of it from subsistence agriculture. When people leave the land and move to the city, life expectancy, education, and incomes rise. Fertility rates decline as women can find work outside of the home and children can go to school rather than working in the fields. Manufacturing and industrialization bring greater societal wealth, infrastructure, and higher wages. By virtually every quantifiable economic, health, education, and environmental metric, life improves when people move to the city, even as it brings new challenges.

Third, we need to accelerate the long-term processes of growing more food on less land. Meeting rising food demand for a global population that will continue to grow for at least the next several decades, without converting virtually all of our remaining forests and grasslands to agriculture, will require that we grow food ever-more efficiently. Making more room for nature will, perhaps counterintuitively, require that we use the land on which we produce food more exclusively for production. A world with more forests, grasslands and wetlands, and more biodiversity within them, will require less biodiversity in our fields.

Finally, raising yields while reducing environmental impacts will require that we farm with ever-greater precision. Raising yields through greater application of technology has often meant more pesticides, fertilizer, and water. But as technology has improved, these trends have begun to reverse. Measured in relationship to agricultural output, nitrogen and water use on US farms has peaked and is now declining. The same is true in other advanced developed economies. Better seeds, irrigation systems, and application practices are allowing for much more precise delivery of inputs when and where plants need them and where they don't. All of those trends will need to be accelerated.

Now, like many people, I am also not immune to the charms of farmer's markets, locally raised grass-fed beef, wild salmon, and all things artisanal. An ecologically vibrant planet in which nine or ten billion people consume healthy diets can also be one in which there is plenty of room for small-scale artisan agriculture and animal husbandry and in which some of us, having been liberated from the land for our sustenance, return to it out of choice. But I think it important that we neither confuse a particular kind of privilege with virtue, nor that we delude ourselves into thinking that these forms of production will be the primary food system that feeds the planet.

I also wonder whether this kind of luxury and artisanship need be so closely tied to our contemporary nostalgia for simplicity and natural foods. By many accounts, the finest beef in the world is raised in Japan, a land-scarce country where kobe beef is raised on beer mash, bathed in sake, massaged daily, and highly confined to prevent the meat from becoming tough. It is not so far from here to laboratory meat, which perhaps someday we might engineer to have similar characteristics. The harvesting of fine caviar has decimated wild sturgeon populations in the Caspian Sea and elsewhere. But thanks to aquaculture technologies developed here at UC Davis, virtually all sturgeon caviar consumed in the United States and Europe is now farmed right here in the Sacramento Delta, and is by all accounts every bit the equal of Russian caviar, if not superior.

Today, some of the finest and most cutting-edge restaurants in the world have begun to serve dishes featuring ants, grasshoppers, and other insects, a vastly more efficient source of protein than most that grace our plates today, and one well suited to high-yield, low-input production. I think it is possible that a prosperous, ecologically vibrant future, characterized by large-scale, high-productivity and high-technology agriculture, might also be one filled with epicurean delights.

The Cattle Industry Could Help Fight Climate Change

Jay Walljasper

Jay Walljasper is a senior fellow at On the Commons, an organization that promotes access to natural resources for all members of society, and is the editor of the organization's website, OnTheCommons.org.

On an unseasonably warm and sunny winter morning—the kind that lulls you into thinking global climate change can't be so bad—a group of environmentalists and sustainable agriculture advocates gather over muffins and coffee on a California ranch to discuss a bold initiative to reverse the greenhouse effect. It's a diverse group—longtime ranchers, a forestry professor from Berkeley, organic food activists, a Vermont dairy farmer, the author of a famous children's book—united in their belief that current proposals to address the climate crisis don't go far enough. On The Commons cofounder Peter Barnes, author of the book *Climate Solutions*, is also on hand along with OTC fellows Ana Micka and myself.

"We now have 380 parts per million of carbon in the atmosphere, compared to 280 before the industrial revolution. Even if we stopped all emissions today, which is a long way from happening, it would still be 345 a century from now," notes John Wick, echoing the sobering conclusions of a report released last year by the UN's Intergovernmental Panel on Climate Change (IPCC), the group awarded the 2007 Nobel Peace Prize along with Al Gore.

Wick—who owns this ranch in the hills of Marin County north of San Francisco with Peggy Rathmann, author of the classic picture book *Goodnight Gorilla*—goes on to outline the climate crisis in terms all-too-familiar to anyone paying attention to the issue. But he then offers a solution that would astonish most people, especially green activists: "Eat a local grass-fed burger."

"It will take carbon out of the air and put it back into the soil," chimes in Abe Collins, the Vermont dairy farmer.

This idea is shocking on two counts:

First, the cattle industry and meat eating are targeted as a leading cause of global warming, up there with autos, jet planes and coal-burning power plants. The animal rights group People for [the] Ethical Treatment of Animals (PETA), for instance, recently launched an ad campaign declaring, "Meat is the No. 1 Cause of Global Warming."

Second, efforts to stop global warming have been focused almost entirely on reducing emissions, not in taking existing carbon out of the atmosphere (a process known as known as carbon sequestration).

Carbon sequestration is not a new idea. It figures prominently in the popular carbon off-setting programs in which people pay a firm to plant trees—which absorb atmospheric carbon in their trunks, branches and roots—to compensate for their carbon emissions from air or auto travel. Coal companies and the Bush Administration have also floated the idea of massive engineering projects to sequester carbon underground, which have been greeted with intense skepticism by most environmentalists due to the cost and the unproven nature of the technology.

But initiatives to sequester carbon in soil through growing crops and grazing animals are less common, but perhaps more promising than planting trees since croplands and grasslands cover more of the earth's surface than forests and they grow at a faster rate.

Scientists agree that organic matter in topsoil is on average 50 percent carbon up to one foot in depth, and bumping that upward by as little as 1.6 percent across all the world's agricultural land, according to John Wick and Abe Collins, would solve the problem of global warming. Soil scientists studying the issue are more measured in their predictions, but still enthusiastic about the potential of soil sequestration of carbon to reduce the threat of global warming.

The central idea of carbon farming is to move the animals frequently—as once happened with wild herds chased by predators—so grasses are not gnawed beyond the point of natural recovery and plant cover remains to fertilize the land and sequester carbon. The sequestration process works like this: The grass takes in carbon from the atmosphere; the animals trample the grass into the soil, where the carbon is absorbed; new grass sprouts and the process is repeated over and over again, absorbing more and more carbon.

This was the natural cycle before the enclosure of the commons. Bison roamed the great American plains, as did other large herds in wild lands throughout the rest of the world. Even in places where livestock farming prevailed, the grazing lands were still held in common and animals wandered freely under the watch of shepherds or small farmers. With the privatization of grazing land, this ecological system was disrupted to the point where today raising livestock is rightly seen as one of the most environmentally destructive industries.

Carbon farming is an attempt to recreate the natural conditions of a commons even under the structure of private property in order to reverse the effects of global climate disruption.

"The idea of soil sequestration is still under the radar," notes Soil Science Professor Chuck Rice of Kansas State University, a member of the IPCC panel who directs a joint project of nine American universities and the US Department of Energy studying the potential for reducing greenhouse gases through agricultural practices. "There is more carbon stored in the soil than in the atmosphere. If we can make a small change in managing that carbon in the soil, it would make a big difference in the atmosphere."

Rice suggests adopting a wide range of carbon sequestration strategies, ranging from planting more trees to cultivating crops using no-till agriculture (which minimizes plowing) to raising animals on grasslands instead of feedlots—the idea that excites

Wick and his fellow ranchers in California. In Canada, a group of power utilities has already signed an agreement with Saskatchewan farmers practicing no-till agriculture to offset the carbon produced by their power plants.

"This isn't wishful thinking down the road," Rice asserts. "It's being done right now and we can do a lot more."

Professor Whendee Silver, a biogeochemist in the Environmental Policy and Management department at the University of California-Berkeley concurs. "Absolutely I think it's possible to sequester carbon in the soil. This is a hot topic of research right now," she says. She just began a study of 36 agricultural fields in California—including John Wick's and Peggy Rathmann's ranch—that are being managed in ways that boost the soil's capacity to absorb carbon.

Wick and Rathmann are running 180 head of cattle on 340 acres using an intricate grazing system designed by Abe Collins to mimic the ecological conditions that occurred when wild bison and elk thundered across the grasslands of North America. They restrict the cattle to a few acres of grassland at a time, moving them as many as four times a day to minimize the effects of overgrazing and to maximize the carbon absorbed by native grasses into the soil—a technique called "carbon farming" or "holistic management." This is based on a theory devised by African game rancher Allan Savory, who believes soil is healthiest and best able to absorb carbon when grasslands are managed in a way similar to the natural cycles created by huge herds of hoofed animals feeding on and trampling grasses for short periods and then moving elsewhere to avoid predators.

Whendee Silver will do extensive chemical analysis of the soil to test the results of these practices. "Many believe the soil has a large potential to sequester carbon—especially degraded soil, which should be able to recoup lost carbon. This could really be a win-win situation, because these soil practices almost always improve the agricultural capacity of the land. And think about the amount of degraded soil around the world."

Silver, Chuck Rice (whose research often takes him to South America) and other researchers see hope for fighting global poverty as well as global warming with these new farming techniques because tropical climates and degraded land, frequently found in the world's poorest nations, have the most potential for sequestering carbon.

Soil Science Professor Rattan Lal, director of the Carbon Management and Sequestration Center at Ohio State University, notes, "The best places are Africa and Asia. But that is where it is hardest to do right now." In an article published in *Science* (Jan. 30, 2008) he and associates say, "Aid programs should place far greater emphasis on subsidizing and providing technical and other assistance for soil restoration."

Lal, a native of India who spent eighteen years at the International Institute of Tropical Agriculture in Nigeria before coming to Ohio State in 1987, advocates an international trading system that would offer lucrative incentives for people in the developing world to undertake no-till farming, sustainable forestry and managed grazing projects that return carbon to soil in significant quantities. "Carbon should be a farm commodity people can buy and sell like any other commodity, then poor farmers would have another income stream," he says.

Abe Collins has launched a trading program along these lines in the US through Carbon Farmers of America, a group he co-founded after seeing remarkable results with carbon farming at his organic dairy farm in Vermont.

Outlining the new trading program, Collins says, "What we are proposing is to pay farmers for their important services that we as a society need—climate regulation, healthy soils." The organization sells offsets for carbon sequestered into the soil (known as a carbon sink) at $25 a ton on its website). Nineteen dollars goes to the farmer, five dollars to public education about carbon farming, and one dollar for the organization's administrative costs.

He estimates that $45 billion in annual payments to farmers sequestering carbon would make the US carbon neutral—not such a high pricetag, Collins muses, when you consider that US taxpayers bailed out the Wall Street trading company Bear Stearns for $30 billion and fork over $31 billion in agriculture subsidies every year to continue current farm policies which degrade the environment and fuel global warming. The $45 billion would also represent an investment in improving soil quality and promoting sustainable agriculture.

Collins originally took the idea of soil carbon trading to the Chicago Climate Exchange—a leader in the idea of organizing financial incentives for businesses practices that reduce greenhouse gases—but they found it too experimental at this point. However soil carbon credits are now being discussed in Australia, according to Collins, which makes sense because carbon farming is more advanced in Australia than anywhere else according to most observers.

A lifelong environmentalist and social justice activist, Collins, 35, grew interested in land restoration while working on the Navajo reservation in Arizona. He returned home to Vermont seven years ago to put his ideas into practice, eventually renting a small farm near St. Albans and joining the Organic Valley dairy cooperative.

A major influence for Collins has been the work of Allan Savory, a trained biologist and game rancher in Zimbabwe who noticed decades ago that land roamed by large herds of antelope or other hooved animals was generally healthy while land managed by farmers or government agencies was often in danger of becoming desert. Savory, who now divides his time between Africa and the New Mexico, formulated a new method of grazing he calls Holistic Management (the foundation of carbon farming), which he says is now practiced on about 30 million acres of grassland in Africa, Australia, and North America.

Following Savory's suggestions, Collins sows native grasses such as timothy, brome, red clover, and ryegrass, which grow as high as two feet tall, on his 135 acres of pasture. He moves his herd of 65 dairy cows to different spots around the pasture five to eight times a day. "The effect is that animals trample the grass onto the land, where it feeds the soil," Collins says, estimating that he has created at least six inches of prime topsoil capable of sequestering substantial amounts of C02 in just three years of carbon farming.

This flies smack in the face of conventional agricultural thinking, which holds that intensive grazing ruins lands and the only way to restore it is by removing animals for a long period of time. "We have land that has been rested for decades and it is still degraded," responds Collins, citing his experience working in the American Southwest.

The central idea in carbon farming is moving the animals frequently—as once happened with wild herds chased by predators—so grasses are not gnawed beyond the point of natural recovery and plant cover remains to fertilize the land and sequester carbon. But many farmers, especially those with large operations, are skeptical of this practice because of the extra labor involved. A major research effort led by Cornell University Professor David Pimentel studying Collins' operation and nineteen other farms in New England, Iowa, Nebraska and California to test the claims and explore the potential of carbon farming is set to [be] slated to begin this summer.

In addition to running his farm, Collins has become a leading advocate for agriculture's role in solving problem of global warming. He's helping John Wick and Peggy Rathmann map out a grazing management plan for the new cattle herd on their California grassland and he's advising the Marin Carbon Project, a new initiative to promote carbon farming as way to lower Marin County's high carbon footprint.

That's what brought Collins to the meeting last February at the California ranch, where he and Wick heralded the hamburger as a savior of the planet.

"The hamburger makes a good symbol of what can be done with carbon farming," Collins says. So he reasons that eating grass-fed beef from sustainably-managed herds will contribute in a small way to reversing global warming. Any large hoofed animals like sheep, goats, bison, elk, antelope or horses can be used in carbon farming, and raising meat isn't essential to the process. Collins after all is a dairy farmer.

But what about the argument that meat-eating is a major cause of global warming due to massive emissions of nitrous oxide, methane and other greenhouse gases from livestock operations? John Wick answers immediately and forcefully, "That's absolutely correct about feedlots and absolutely wrong about grass-fed livestock. Sustainably-raised grass-fed beef is a natural system and the methane and other greenhouse gases are mitigated by the carbon sequestration in the soil. We see this as a way to phase out feedlots." Collins adds that nitrous oxides are in huge part the product of chemical fertilizers, which don't make any sense in a farming system based on restoring the soil and halting global warming.

On The Commons' Peter Barnes is looking into the idea of carbon farming. "We saw the Arctic melt last summer and Greenland glaciers slide into the ocean," he says, "and scientists realize that climate change is happening faster than in their models. We seem to be a tipping point right now, and that's the context for ideas like carbon farming and planting trees. Sequestration is not a marginal idea but central to any effort [to] keep the planet from tipping into disaster."

One reason why carbon farming and other sequestration methods have gotten far less attention in the fight against global warming than efforts to reduce emissions is because they represent something new in environmental policy—the idea that solving our ecological crisis means not just stopping human interference with nature, but also on humans taking positive steps to undo the damage already here.

"The days of hands-off environmentalism are over," declares John Wick. "Humans are part of nature, we are part of ecosystems. We can be part of the solution.

"If the solution to global warming involves large herds of hoofed animals moving through landscape in ways that take carbon out of the atmosphere and into the soil, we can do that."

Wick notes that when he and Rathmann first bought their ranch, they stopped leasing the land to neighboring cattle farmers in the belief that livestock was an unnatural element imposed upon the land by humans, which threatened the healthy ecosystem of these fragile, rolling hills. "We are environmentalists and thought the best thing to do was kick the cows off, and when we did that we watched the coyote bush—a natural plant that takes over when there are no animals to eat it—kill all the other vegetation on our hills."

In late March, they welcomed cattle back to their ranch and within a week reported enthusiastically that their brown hillsides were already turning green.

CHAPTER 4

Does the Industrial Food Complex Increase Economic Inequality?

The Food System Is Inextricably Linked to Wider Struggles in Economic Inequality and Systemic Racism

Anna Brones

Anna Brones is the editor of Foodie Underground. *Her work has been featured in the* New York Times, *BBC, the* Guardian, *and other publications.*

America's sustainable food movement has been steadily growing, challenging consumers to truly consider where our food comes from, and inspiring people to farm, eat local, and rethink our approaches to food policy. But at the same time, the movement is predominantly white, and often neglects the needs and root problems of diverse communities.

Issues of economic inequality and systemic racism permeate our national food system. The movement's primary focus has been on finding solutions to "food deserts"—defined as areas empty of good-quality, affordable fresh food—by working to ensure that affected neighborhoods have better access. But some advocates, and studies, have argued that the proximity of a well-stocked grocery store is not enough of a solution given this country's elaborate food problems.

Farm subsidies in the United States go predominantly to white farmers, which has led a group of black farmers to sue the US government for discrimination. Food pantries, which distribute food directly to those in need, are stigmatized. Our subsidized food system, as the activist and community organizer Karen Washington points out in the interview that follows, "skews the cost and value of food."

Washington has been battling for food justice for three decades. Before taking up the cause, she worked as a physical therapist, and saw many of her patients, predominantly people of color, suffering from diabetes, obesity, and hypertension. (More than one-third of American adults, and 48% of African American adults, are obese.) Treatment always involved medication and surgery as opposed to prevention, and Washington knew there had to be a better way. She moved to the Bronx, in New York, in the mid-1980s and became a vocal community gardener.

Since that time, Washington has won a James Beard Foundation Leadership Award, been invited to the Obama White House for her involvement with New York's Botanical Garden, and been called "urban farming's de facto godmother." She's also worked to transform the Bronx's empty lots into spaces where food can grow, helped launch a farmers' market, and, in relentlessly engaging her community, has remained focused on the intersections of food and issues like poverty, racism, a lack of healthcare, and joblessness.

In other words, Washington has been around the block. What she found is that there weren't very many people who looked like her with active roles in the food system. To bring additional voices to the table, she cofounded Black Urban Growers, an organization dedicated to supporting and advocating for black farmers and black leadership in the food movement, in 2009. And as she creates a more inclusive food community, she is working to redefine the challenges that the food system faces, too. Washington is opposed to using the expression "food desert," which she calls "an outsider term" that calls desolate places, rather than places with enormous potential, to mind. She prefers "food apartheid," which "brings us to the more important question: what are some of the social inequalities that you see, and what are you doing to erase some of the injustices?"

Guernica: When did you begin growing food?

Karen Washington: Well, it all started with a tomato. I never liked it. It wasn't red, it was pale pink, it had no taste. Until I started growing it myself, I didn't even know it grew on a vine, let alone that it was red and brown and juicy. When I finally bit into someone's fresh, garden-grown tomato, it just changed my world. It really gave me the ambition to want to grow food myself. Then, in 1988, I looked out my kitchen window to the empty lot across the way and saw a man with a pick and a shovel. I went out and I asked him what he was doing, and he said, "I'm thinking about starting a community garden." I asked if I could help. We're about to celebrate our 30th year [of working together].

Guernica: That's amazing!

Karen Washington: It is amazing. My gardening got me into community organizing and activism. I noticed that when I went to visit friends who were white, their neighborhoods, their food system, their supermarkets were totally different compared to what I was seeing in my backyard. At my local supermarkets, things that should have been composted were wrapped up in cellophane and sold at a reduced price. We had a variety of food, but I wouldn't call it fresh. It looked like it was secondhand, and people had no other options.

I eventually realized that I couldn't concentrate on food alone because there were so many things that were intersecting. I saw that the people who were in [that first community] garden were mostly low-income and had no health insurance. The garden wasn't just being used for food, but also for wellbeing and medicine. The healthcare industry is part of this conversation. As a physical therapist, I used to see billions more spent on treatment than prevention. Look at the pharmaceutical companies. In my neighborhood, there is a fast-food restaurant on every block, from Wendy's to Kentucky Fried Chicken to Popeye's to Little Caesar's Pizza. Now drugstores are popping up on every corner, too. So you have the fast-food restaurants that of course cause the diet-related diseases, and you have the pharmaceutical companies there to fix it. They go hand in hand. The fact is, if you do prevention, someone is going to lose money. If you give people access to really good food and a living-wage job, someone is going to lose money.

As long as people are poor and as long as people are sick, there are jobs to be made. Follow the money.

I set out on this journey to explain the conditions of impoverishment. A lot of these communities need an influx of resources and monetary help, along with more local ownership of land and capital, in order to change things around. I go around the country to challenge people to see beyond the "raised beds" and to recognize that we live in one of the greatest nations and countries of all time and yet we still suffer from hunger and poverty. How have we allowed that to happen and what are we going to do to change that?

Guernica: We often use the expression "food desert" today. Does that term help us create infrastructure to ensure better access to food, or is it hindering our ability to do so?

Karen Washington: I was just in Pennsylvania and North Carolina talking about food deserts, and the topic of food justice and food sovereignty, and putting it out there that it means nothing to me. I asked people to define it, and, of course, they gave me their cookie-cutter definition: "Communities who have limited access to food." That means nothing. Who in in my actual neighborhood has deemed that we live in a food desert? Number one, people will tell you that they do have food. Number two, people in the hood have never used that term. It's an outsider term. "Desert" also makes us think of an empty, absolutely desolate place. But when we're talking about these places, there is so much life and vibrancy and potential. Using that word runs the risk of preventing us from seeing all of those things.

What I would rather say instead of "food desert" is "food apartheid," because "food apartheid" looks at the whole food system, along with race, geography, faith, and economics. You say "food apartheid" and you get to the root cause of some of the problems around the food system. It brings in hunger and poverty. It brings us to the more important question: What are some of the social inequalities that you see, and what are you doing to erase some of the injustices?

So, now, let's go a little further; let's talk about food sovereignty. Food sovereignty is being coopted in the same way that food justice is, because "food sovereignty" was a term that was really founded by indigenous people in Central and South America when they were fighting for governance. The organization Via Campesina coined the term "food sovereignty." They were fighting for land ownership and they were fighting for resiliency, so we should make sure that we pay respect to those indigenous people who have been fighting for so long. "Food sovereignty" is now being interchanged with "food justice", and although they are coexisting conditions, they are two terms with substantial differences. Even those terms have been watered down, but "food desert" sugarcoats what the problem is. If you bring a supermarket in, it's not going to change the problem. When we say "food apartheid," the real conversation can begin.

Guernica: You mentioned wanting to challenge people to look beyond their raised beds. What is the best way to ensure that people have access to food? Is it by focusing on food production or focusing on systemic racism and economics?

Karen Washington: All of the above. This idea that just because you give people the ability to grow their own food, and give up soda for water, that all of [a] sudden it's going to make these people's conditions better? No. We have to talk about race, we have to talk about economics, because those are the things holding people back.

I wake up dreaming that my neighborhood has been given capital, has been given opportunity, has been given finance, that we can own our stores and businesses. Why is it that outsiders always have to come into our neighborhood to open a business? Why don't people with capital come into my neighborhood and think about investing in the people who already live here? Give them the capital, give them the means of financial literacy, teach them how to invest, teach them how to own homes, teach them how to own businesses. Give them that chance, instead of coming in and changing the dynamics and the complexion of our neighborhood.

People often interview me and they ask me questions like: what's it like to live in a neighborhood with limited access to food? After a while, I shut it down. I say, "Why don't you turn it around?" Because I want to hear what people in affluent neighborhoods are doing. What is their take on people who live in food deserts? What is the conversation that rich, white, privileged people have about poverty and hunger and what are they doing to make a change? Sit down at the table with a family member, a father, a mother, who owns a business, and ask them what they're doing to ensure that their businesses are employing people who need jobs, or [ask if] they're getting out of their comfort zone, not just writing a check, because it's easy to write a check, but what are they doing to invest in neighborhoods that are less fortunate?

Guernica: I've moved back to my hometown, a rural community where we have high poverty rates and many kids receive free school lunches. We do have a food bank and other programs that provide access to fresh food, and it's easy for people to write a check to a food bank or buy a couple cans of food to donate, but it feels like a Band-Aid on a larger problem.

Karen Washington: It is a Band-Aid. I recently asked [the students in my gardening] classes, "What is the purpose of food pantries and food kitchens?" And of course they say, "To feed the poor," and "to have access to food," and so on. But the main function of these two approaches is [supposed to be] that they're reserved for emergencies only. Instead, they've become a way of life.

How do we sit with the fact that 40 million people are in poverty? The system of giving out free food is not going to fix that. Even as a farmer, I have to deal with the fact that when I come down to the farmers' market and sell my produce I have to educate people about the value and cost of food, because I am surrounded by a food system—a subsidized food system—that skews the cost and value of food. My carrots are $2. They are $2 because I am a for-profit farmer, and unlike the carrot for 99 cents that's sold in cellophane at the supermarket down the street or the bunch of carrots that you got for free from the food pantry, this two-dollar carrot is feeding me, my family, and it means something.

The conversation around actual food value is a conversation that we don't have in low-income neighborhoods, regardless if they're black or white, rural or urban. But things are changing. People are talking more than ever about food. It's such a major shift, so you're seeing major corporations offering different options, like fast-food chains offering salads. The consumer is starting to understand the relationship between food and health. It's also happening in low-income communities. The rise in school gardens impacts children and they shift their parents' perspectives. In my neighborhood, every year, we have a block party and they don't serve soda anymore. The kids are asking for water! Education is working.

Guernica: Would it be more advantageous for us to restructure the charity system?

Karen Washington: Yes! First of all, let's think in terms of labeling and messaging. Food pantries are stigmatized. When you say "food pantries," you're talking about people who are poor, standing in line, getting their food as a handout. The organization West Side Campaign Against Hunger has a pantry that they have started to rebrand. They set up their organization like a supermarket, so customers are coming and they're shopping like they would at a regular store. It's not a food pantry where you're giving out free plastic bags of food. They also offer job training, and a chef who teaches the clients if they want to learn how to prepare food.

I tell them to ask people, "Why are you here? What is causing you to be on this food line? Is it the fact that you don't have a job? Are you ill? Are you homeless?" By knowing those answers, they can help a person. For a problem like, "Well, I was homeless, so I am in a food pantry," they talk about what we offer in terms of social work and helping people get apartments. For, "Oh, I just got out of jail," they talk about some of the entry programs out there that can help them. Or: "I lost a job … I'm looking for a job." Let's have job training on site for employment opportunities so people can seek jobs.

Guernica: You launched the Black Urban Growers organization because you had traveled around and hadn't seen anyone else who looked like you in the food movement, which I can imagine felt like a desolate, lonely place.

Karen Washington: That's accurate. I recently went to the Organic Grower's Conference, which is in its 25th year, and someone told me that it was the second year that they had speakers of color. The second year! I don't know how many attendees they had, but I can tell you offhand it was less than maybe seven people of color. And these are food conferences. I ask people about the work that they do, and a lot of them say, "Yeah, we work on a community farm," "We work in a community garden," "You know, it's full of vegetables and flowers," and I say, "You know what? Even within the work that you do with flowers and vegetables, you see diversity. But when it comes to the movement, it's not diverse." How can you see beauty and diversity in the food system, and yet these workshops and conferences are all homogenized? There is no diversity, there's no inclusion.

That's why we have the Black Urban Growers Conference. It's because no one talks about our issues, and when they do talk about our issues it's from a white voice. Why does the respected [one] always have to be a white voice?

People talk about food justice, but where are the farmers who look like me and who were brought here as slaves to do agriculture? When I asked that question, I was told, "Black people don't want to farm, all they want to do is play basketball and play music." When people tell me that, I know I am doing the right thing with this work.

For me and my friends, it has been inspirational. People come up to me at the end of the conference and say that they have never seen so many black farmers in a room. They have never had a conference that presented issues that pertained to the black experience.

Guernica: Why do you think food conferences don't give people of color a platform?

Karen Washington: They're not taking the time to go out of their comfort zones to reach people. That's the bottom line. The reason I attend conferences is because people reach out and invite me. I'm going to write to Organic Growers and give them a list of people of color that they need to reach out to. Some of those people include: Leah Penniman, Malik Yakini, Lorrie Clevenger, Dr. Gale Myers, Kirtrina Baxter, Keisha Cameron, Kelly Carlisle, and Chris Newsome. I asked people in the African American community if they were going to that conference and they said they weren't invited. That's the problem. People live in their silos.

I also have a problem with organizations in urban areas and communities of color that are white-led. You started an organization and you have been there for 10 or 15 years and your mission statement says that one day the people within the community will have leadership. They should have your job right now; why are you still there? I talk about power, and how power is a drug and power over people is a drug and it's hard to give up. But once you start taking a job in a community, and particularly a community of color, once you are there as the emergency department, you should be thinking about how you are going to transition out.

Guernica: In the sense that a desert is an "empty" place, do you feel that the food movement has become a "desert"?

Karen Washington: At the conference, it's also powerful to hear young people talk about reparations and going back to the land. The younger black farming community is growing. Leah Penniman of Soul Fire Farm is doing excellent work. Young people are understanding the power that they have and they are not waiting for us to fix it. Look at Black Lives Matter; they are very outspoken. They are unapologetic. They know what's right. They know the oppression and segregation and the racism that have happened and continue to happen. They're not drinking the Kool-Aid.

Even still, the average age of a farmer is 59. The movement is going to be a desert if we don't get more youth involved. Who is out there? How are we going to get the next wave of farmers? The price of land for new farmers is crazy. So how do we entice a new generation to become farmers if they don't have access to land? They have credit-card and student-loan debt, and there's no diversity to encourage the young blood of new farmers with different faces to come into the food system.

Guernica: The food movement has essentially become a monocrop.

Karen Washington: Exactly. As we know, you lose diversity and it will truly end up a desert because you've never taken the time to nourish that seed, diversify that seed, and you kept doing the same thing over and over again. And you know what happens when you continue to grow in the same soil? It gets depleted of nutrients and becomes barren. That's what's going to happen to the food movement if we don't think about planting seeds of diversity, of new young blood, into the food system.

Agricultural Dumping Increases Income Inequality Worldwide

Sophia Murphy and Karen Hansen-Kuhn

Sophia Murphy serves as the Senior Advisor for the Institute for Agriculture & Trade Policy. She works on agricultural trade rules, US trade and agriculture policy, and food security. Karen Hansen-Kuhn is the Director of Trade and Global Governance for the Institute for Agriculture & Trade Policy. Her focus is on trade and economic justice.

The Trump administration is threatening to crack down on foreign steel producers who are allegedly dumping cheap steel into the US market. "Dumping," the practice of exporting goods at prices lower than in the country where the goods are produced, is widely considered an unfair way to gain foreign market share.

But you're unlikely to hear Trump officials complain about dumping in agricultural trade because in this sector, it's the US exporters who are at fault.

The Institute for Agriculture and Trade Policy (IATP) has used World Trade Organization formulas to document the systematic dumping of US grown agricultural commodities (specifically wheat, soybeans, corn, cotton, and rice) for two decades. They found that in the wake of the volatile commodity markets that dominated in the period from 2007 to 2013, export prices largely exceeded production costs. In recent years, however, US agricultural commodity dumping has started again. According to IATP's calculations, in 2015 US wheat was exported at 32 percent less than the cost of production, soybeans at 10 percent less, corn at 12 percent less, and rice at 2 percent less.

Dumping clearly increases inequality between farmers in the global North and South. Less visibly, dumping also worsens incomes and increases inequality within rural America.

For the farmers who grow the same (or substitutable) crops in the importing countries, agricultural dumping makes it nearly impossible to make a profit. It is especially devastating for such farmers in low-income countries, where governments have no means to provide compensation, nor the economic power to use trade rules to defend their markets.

Dumping creates unfair competition for producers in other exporting countries, too. And by encouraging overproduction in the United States, dumping traps US producers as well, forcing them to engage in a never-ending push for higher yields or bigger farms, or both.

The biggest winners from dumping are the handful of agricultural commodity trading corporations that dominate the markets (four corporations control an estimated 75-90 percent of the global grain trade). Their enormous market power allows these agribusinesses to squeeze small farmers and consumers, keeping the vast majority of profits for themselves. Farmers typically earn just a few pennies out of each dollar of food their grain goes into making.

Farmers do make a profit some years. But many other years farmers work at a loss, while agribusinesses make money much more consistently. When we look at the cost of production and the movement to ports and then to export, there are profits and losses at various stages but much of it is hidden behind vertically integrated supply chains, for example when grain traders own feedlots or when poultry producers contract with farmers to control the breeding and raising of chickens while also controlling the processing and marketing.

Corporate concentration in nearly every sector of agricultural inputs, production, processing and distribution has increased substantially over the last 20 years. The system is structured in a way that allows, even encourages, farmers to operate at a loss, which maximizes profits further downstream for agribusiness and leaves the public covering the farmers' losses.

The current US Farm Bill, the omnibus agricultural legislation passed every five years, includes revenue insurance programs that respond to price drops, but they are not designed to resolve them. They compensate farmers to some degree for the catastrophic drop in farm prices, even as costs have continued to rise. They do nothing to slow or lessen production. Farm incomes have plummeted for the last three years, and the level of farm debt as a share of farm income is the highest since the 1980s.

The US government's answer has been to encourage even more exports to compensate for low prices. The value of revenue insurance will also diminish over time as its value is calculated by a moving average of prices that are now, once again, decreasing. The fall in revenue will increase the political pressure on Congress to introduce "emergency measures," as has happened often in the past. Such financial bail-outs, while providing much needed relief, do nothing to redress the market inequalities between producers on the one hand and farm input companies, grain traders, and processors on the other.

One of the countries hardest hit by unfair competition with US agricultural exports is Mexico. Corn holds an important place in Mexico's economy, diet, and culture. Under the 1994 North American Free Trade Agreement (NAFTA), US corn exports to Mexico increased more than 400 percent in the first few years, disrupting local markets. Based on Mexican Census data, Tim Wise estimates that more than two million Mexicans left agriculture in the wake of NAFTA's flood of imports, or as many as one quarter of the farming population. Even when dumping rates decreased during the period of high prices, existing public support programs for agriculture in Mexico, as in the United States, tended to support the largest farmers and agribusiness interests, rather than the smaller producers who had been the backbones of their rural economies.

The Mexican government has responded to the Trump administration's calls to renegotiate—or abandon—NAFTA by seeking to diversify its sources of corn imports. One proposal in the Mexican Senate calls for the government to cease corn imports from the United States and instead purchase from Brazil, in effect substituting imports from one set of agribusinesses to another.

The big grain traders have also profited from new technologies, such as the computer-driven high frequency trading that now dominates financial markets and has amplified commodity price swings. These firms are in the business of adding value to primary commodities, whether they are fattening animals or turning corn into ethanol. Cheap grain then becomes an input, and the companies are happy to keep those prices low. The structure of those supply chains, as well as the rules that govern them, favor agribusinesses with global reach.

What's the solution? Several US food and farm groups see the re-opening of the NAFTA debate as an opportunity to challenge the enormous power of the big agribusiness corporations. In early 2017 they issued a call for a different approach to the trade deal—one that allows countries to "protect their farmers from unfair imports that distort the domestic market, undermine prices, and ultimately compromise the economic viability of independent farmers."

There is an urgent need for a new approach to global trade rules—an approach that respects the obligation on governments to protect food security at home, the complex relationship of food systems to economic development, and the importance of accountability in domestic politics in rich and poor countries alike. Prices must incorporate environmental costs as well and allow for sustainable resource use. It is time for strong, clear rules that value more equitable returns to food production and distribution throughout the supply chain, as well as stable and predictable food prices.

Agribusiness Employs Undocumented Immigrants at Unlivable Wages

Sadhbh Walshe

Sadhbh Walshe is a filmmaker and contributor to the Guardian. *She worked on the CBS drama series* The District *and has published pieces in the* Chicago Tribune *and* Irish Times.

This week, a bipartisan group of senators and the president unveiled their respective plans for much needed and long overdue immigration reform. For the 11 million or so undocumented immigrants who have settled in this country, the path to citizenship being paved for them looks like it will be more tough than fair.

While we don't yet know how this will all play out, at least there will be a path. For one group of immigrants, however—the farm workers who sustain our food supply—there is reason to fear that what awaits them is not a path to citizenship, but their cemented status as indentured servants.

Most farm work in America is performed by immigrants, most of whom are undocumented and therefore exploitable. The big agribusinesses that hire these immigrants will tell you that they need an unfettered supply of cheap foreign labor, because they cannot find Americans willing to do these jobs.

When you consider what these jobs entail—hours of backbreaking work in terrible and often dangerous conditions, subsistence wages with little or no time off, and none of the protections or perks that most of us enjoy (like paid sick days, for instance)—it's hard to see why anyone with other options would subject themselves to a life that is barely a step above slavery.

In the 1980s, President Ronald Reagan signed a bill into law which introduced some protections for these imported serfs,

"Field Work's Dirty Secret: Agribusiness Exploitation of Undocumented Labor," by Sadhbh Walshe, Guardian News and Media Limited, January 31, 2013. Reprinted by permission.

under what has become known as the guest-worker program. These protections include a minimum wage guarantee, housing that meets an acceptable standard for the duration of the contract, and a guarantee that the worker be paid three-quarters of their full pay should a season end early.

Most employers would be delighted to get away with all this: being able to hire low-wage workers at will, without the hassle of paying disability insurance or other niceties. But agribusinesses find the guest-worker program's pitiful protections such a burden that they have mounted a relentless campaign to undermine them, and for the most part, work around them anyway; they hire undocumented workers instead.

According to a report compiled by Eric Ruark, the director of research at the Federation for American Immigration Reform (Fair), as of 2006, only 27% of workers hired by agribusinesses are American citizens, 21% are green card holders, around 1% are part of the guest worker program … and a whopping 51% are unauthorized immigrants.

It's agriculture's worst kept secret that farm owners routinely break the law by hiring undocumented workers, but the crime receives tacit approval from lawmakers sympathetic to the plight of major agribusinesses, which seem to consider cheap labor their right. In South Carolina, for instance, lawmakers passed their version of Arizona's draconian bill, and have mandated that employers use an e-verify system to check the immigration status of employees. Farm workers, however, were exempted from verification.

The agribusiness sector has gotten away with exploitative and illegal practices because of ridiculous threats, like the suggestion that should the supply of cheap labor dry up in the US, they will outsource our food production to China. This idle threat is based on the absurd notion that if they have to pay workers higher wages, somehow there will be fewer people willing to do the jobs. The other scare tactic is spreading talk that if they have to increase their expenditure on labor, those costs will have to be passed on to the American consumer.

Several studies have been conducted, however, that expose these hollow threats for the nonsense that they are. A report by the Congressional Research Service found no evidence of a labor shortage in the agricultural sector. On the contrary, it found that between 1994 and 2008, the unemployment rate for farm workers was consistently higher than for all other occupations. In other words, agriculture has had a surplus of available workers for decades.

During this period, the agricultural industry has recorded a nearly 80% average annual increase in profits—more than all other major industries. No doubt, these record profits have something to do with the fact that real wages for farm workers have remained stagnant throughout this time. Finally, a 2011 report by the Economic Policy Institute found that an increase in farm workers' wages of 40% would result in an annual rise in household spending by the American consumer of just $16.

Clearly, the economic argument for allowing one industry a workforce of virtually indentured labor does not hold water. But there is a humanitarian argument to be made, as well, that should be enough to put an end to this exploitative practice immediately. In 2009, the *New York Times'* Bob Herbert wrote an article about the horrible treatment of farm workers in upstate New York—in this case, hired to feed and care for ducks farmed to be slaughtered for foie gras.

> "The routine is brutal and not very sanitary. Each feeding takes about four hours and once the birds are assigned a feeder, no one else can be substituted during the 22 day force feeding period that leads up to the slaughter … Not only do the feeders get no days off during that long stretch, and no overtime for any of the long hours, but they get very little time even to sleep each day. The feeding schedule for the ducks must be rigidly observed.

"When I asked one of the owners, Izzy Yanay, about the lack of a day of rest, he said of the workers: 'This notion that they need to rest is completely futile. They don't like to rest. They want to work seven days.'"

Herbert went on to make the point that we are much more likely to hear complaints about cruelty to ducks by force-feeding than we are about the cruelty to the people hired to feed them. Consumers have long since showed a willingness to pay more for organic meat or chicken because they don't like the idea of animal cruelty.

Are we really not willing to pay a few cents more for farm produce so that human beings are not treated like animals?

It remains to be seen what the bipartisan "gang of eight" senators have in mind specifically for farm workers in any future immigration bill. But one can only hope that they will not give in to bullying by the spoiled agricultural industry, which continues to deny these workers the same rights and protections every other worker in America enjoys.

The Fast Food Industry Profits Off of Struggling Workers

Katey Troutman

Katey Troutman is a writer for the Cheat Sheet, *a lifestyle site that covers topics from current political debates to local culture and cuisine.*

There are more than 3.5 million fast-food workers in the United States, and many of them think they're getting the short end of the stick. A nationwide campaign to raise minimum wage, primarily made up of fast food workers, has been ongoing for more than a year. And McDonald's workers made headlines when, in some places, protestors were demanding wages as high as $15 an hour. Wage stagnation has certainly hit most Americans hard, but for workers in low-wage industries, supporters argue, the stagnation has become downright punishing, making every day a struggle.

But is pay disparity in the fast food industry really as bad as protestors claim? Can fast food companies even afford to pay workers higher wages? Let's break down the data. How much do fast food workers make now? About $9.00 an hour, though the most unfortunate make just $8.18 an hour, or about $17,000 a year. Compare that to the average annual wage across the United States, which was about $44,000 in 2013, according to the Social Security Administration, or almost three times what the average fast-food worker makes in a year.

In a word, yes, it does seem that minimum wage workers are getting a pretty shitty deal. But how well is the fast food industry at large doing, anyway? Well, last year, the fast food industry brought in revenues of more than $190 billion, a figure that is expected

"Is the Fast-Food Industry Driving Income Inequality in America?" by Katey Troutman, *The Cheat Sheet*, December 29, 2014. Reprinted by permission.

to rise to more than $210 billion by 2018, and you'll notice that there is something of a "disparity" between the revenue and wage when it comes to fast food. In fact, according to Statista, the cost of wages for the fast food industry remains just 24 percent of the industry's revenue.

Okay, but what about the argument that, in an industry with such slim profit margins, fast food companies really can't *afford* to pay their employees any better. This makes a lot of sense; if a fast food company isn't making much profit in the first place, the company's hands are effectively tied.

As it turns out, though, fast food companies are doing pretty well; yes, the margins are fairly thin, but they're only getting better. Profit margins for privately held fast food companies are currently 4.6 percent, up from 2.1 percent in 2009. Meanwhile, the percentage of revenue spent on payroll has effectively *decreased* from 23.5 percent to 22.9 percent in 2013, according to data from Sageworks. So while it's true that the fast food industry does have slimmer profit margins than many other industries, increasing revenues seem to have gone straight into executive's pocketbooks, while wages for workers have continued to remain stagnant.

Catherine Ruetschlin, a senior policy analyst who authored a recent study on pay disparity conducted by Demos, a public policy organization based in New York, notes that pay disparity is largely the result of "two factors: escalating payments to corporate CEOs and stagnant poverty-level wages received by typical workers in the industry."

In the study, Ruetschlin found that the fast-food industry is one of the major drivers of large-scale pay disparity in the United States. Ruetschlin writes that the accommodation and food services sector, to which the fast-food industry belongs, "was the most unequal sector of the economy in almost every year from 2000 to 2012." She adds that, "Pay disparity at companies in the fast-food industry drove this result, with CEO-to-worker compensation ratios from 2009 to 2012 that were nearly twice those of nearly every other sector."

Pay disparity is an ongoing problem in America, and CEO to worker pay ratios are largely getting worse across the board, but when it comes to the fast food industry, the situation is at its most dismal. For instance, according to the watchdog group, Executive Paywatch the CEO-to-worker pay ratio was 331:1 in 2013. For minimum wage workers, the pay ratio is still worse at 774:1, but for fast food workers, pay disparity is so stark it's almost a little sickening. According to Ruetschlin, "in 2012, the CEO-to-worker compensation ratio in fast-food topped 1,200-to-1. Further, the CEO average pay since 2000 has more than quadrupled, while fast-food workers' wages have increased just 0.3 percent since the new millennium.

Fast-food CEOs are among the highest paid workers in America. According to Ruetschlin, the average fast-food CEO currently makes about $23.8 million a year, more than 500 times the overall average annual wage in the US, and more than 1,300 times the average annual wage of a fast-food worker.

As a result, many fast-food workers struggle to get by; a study conducted last year by economists at the University of California, Berkeley concluded that more than 52% of fast-food workers rely on taxpayer-funded public assistance programs, such as SNAP (otherwise known as food stamps) or Medicaid. These programs (SNAP and Medicaid, along with income eligible tax credits) cost taxpayers an estimated $7 billion annually. Essentially, the Berkeley economists argue, the government is helping to subsidize corporate profits because employees of these companies are unable to sustain themselves without taxpayers assistance.

"The taxpayer costs we discovered were staggering," says Ken Jacobs, of the Center for Labor Research and Education at the University of California Berkeley. "People who work in fast-food jobs are paid so little that having to rely on public assistance is the rule, rather than the exception, even for those working 40 hours or more a week," Jacobs added.

In total, taxpayers contributed a total of about $7 billion in public assistance programs for fast-food workers, and frontline fast-food workers are enrolled in public assistance programs at more than twice the rate of the overall workforce. Medicaid and Children's Health Insurance Program (CHIP) costs account for most of that $7 billion, coming in at about $3.9 billion; less than 13% of fast-food jobs provide healthcare benefits of any kind, the UC Berkeley study found. A similar study conducted by the National Employment Law Project found that McDonald's workers alone received $1.2 billion in public assistance from taxpayers.

"This is the public cost for low-wage jobs in America," said UC Berkeley economist Sylvia Allegretto, one of the authors of the study. "The cost is public because taxpayers bear it. Yet it remains hidden in national policy debates about poverty, employment and public spending."

Further, fast-food workers are often trapped in lower-wage jobs because, despite what the company might claim, there is rarely room for advancement within the industry. "The truth is that millions of fast-food workers will never have an opportunity to move beyond front-line jobs. That's why it's so critical that instead of empty promises of future possibilities, the industry act to ensure that the jobs most fast-food workers occupy provide the wages and benefits workers need to support themselves and their families," said Christine Owens, executive director of the National Employment Law Project, in a press release.

The UC Berkeley study has also helped to dispel many myths about the kinds of people who are employed by fast-food companies. For instance, the majority of the fast-food industry's workers are middle aged—not teenagers living with their parents. Further, more than 60% of fast-food workers are the main income earners in their families, and about a quarter are parents supporting at least one child.

But some conservative economists argue that raising the minimum wage will have unforeseen consequences: for one, companies would most certainly raise the price of your burger and fries, possibly by as much as 30 to 50%, according to Michael Strain, an economist at the American Enterprise Institute. Conservative economists also believe that the fast-food industry is likely to cut jobs if it is forced to raise wages, and given that the industry employs some three and half million people, it's easy to see Strain's point.

Strain says that he doesn't see fast-food workers' reliance on public assistance as a bad thing. "In general, the government is making sure these peoples' basic needs are met, which is an appropriate role of government."

Meanwhile, other economists argue that the fast-food industry's revenues leave plenty of room for a wage increase. "McDonald's profits were $5.6 billion last year," said Jack Temple, an economist at the National Employment Law Project. "There's plenty of revenue to afford a living wage."

Ken Jacobs, one of the authors of the UC Berkeley study, agrees. He adds that raising wages also helps reduce worker turnover, which is good for the company as well as the workers. What the companies lose in profits by raising wages they can potentially gain in cost-savings by keeping their workers longer.

Ruetschlin says that raising fast-food workers wages won't just allow working families to maintain a better quality of living without having to rely on public assistance, but could also help improve fast-food companies' bottom line. "Reducing the proportion of CEO-to-worker compensation by addressing bad practices on both halves of the ratio is one step toward realigning the interests of stakeholders in the firm, including shareholders, executives, and the workforce overall."

McDonald's, for one, has begun to take notice of the risk associated with pay disparity. In a January SEC filing, the company listed protests by its low wage workers, increasing awareness of income inequality, and public perception of working conditions at the company's franchises among the risks to shareholders in the upcoming year. Further, in June of 2014, McDonald's CEO Don Thompson suggested in a speech at Northwestern University's Kellogg School of Management that he supports a minimum wage increase. "We will support any legislation that moves forward," Thompson said, per the *Chicago Tribune* adding that "McDonald's will be fine. We'll manage through whatever additional cost implications there are." "Managing" certainly sounds better than what most of the companies' front-line workers are doing.

Agribusiness Can Promote International Economic Development and Sustainability

Catherine Ward

Catherine Ward received her master's degree in environmental science from Rhodes University. Her primary research interest is global food security.

Agriculture employs more than one billion people worldwide—about 34 percent of global workers—making it the second-largest source of employment globally. Yet agricultural workers remain one of the most marginalized, oppressed, and exploited groups in the world. According to a report by the UN Food and Agriculture Organization (FAO), the International Labor Organization (ILO), and International Union of Food, Agriculture, Hotel, Restaurant, Catering, Tobacco, and Allied Workers' Associations (IUF), the global agricultural workforce is "among the most socially vulnerable; the least organized into trade unions; employed under the poorest health, safety and environmental conditions; and is the least likely to have access to effective forms of social security and protection."

In many countries, up to 60 percent of agricultural workers live in poverty and less than 20 percent have access to basic social security, according to the Sustainable Agriculture and Rural Development (SARD) initiative. The agricultural sector also has the largest numbers of child workers—nearly 130 million children between the ages of 5 and 17.

Innovations to lift the world's agricultural workers out of poverty can simultaneously promote sustainable agriculture and international development. Today, Nourishing the Planet offers six solutions to help lift the world's agricultural workers out of poverty:

"Six Innovations Lifting the World's Agricultural Workers Out of Poverty," by Catherine Ward, Worldwatch Institute. Reprinted by permission.

Support Organized Labor

Labor unions play an important role in minimizing exploitation among agricultural workers by advocating for higher wages, improved living conditions, and safer work environments. Agricultural workers are often one of the most disempowered groups within societies, and in many countries they lack access to basic healthcare, education, and participation in government. Unions advocate for worker rights, and fight to stop the exploitation of children.

In Ghana, 70 percent of the country's 23 million inhabitants are involved in the agricultural sector. The General Agricultural Workers Union (GAWU) is the largest union in Ghana and represents many marginalized agricultural groups. The union supports rural communities by providing support in training, learning new skills, and microcredit. GAWU is currently investing in a youth development center, and organizes training workshops for union members. The union has campaigned for better farm wages, so that families don't have to send their children to work in the agricultural sector.

By supporting community-based organizations, such as the Coalition of Immokalee Workers (CIW), consumers in the United States can help ensure that farmworker's rights are recognized and enforced. The CIW is a coalition of farmworkers working low-wage jobs in the state of Florida, and is responsible for advocating farmworker rights via hunger strikes, boycotts, interfaith prayer vigils, rallies, and marches. The CIW is organizing a Labor Day Weekend of Action and is calling on the public to actively protest Publix in your state.

Include Women in Agricultural Development

Innovative technology solutions can help disadvantaged agricultural workers ease their work burdens and increase productivity. Women make up over 40 percent of the global agricultural workforce, yet are one of the most vulnerable groups amongst these workers. Female agricultural laborers form an invisible workforce, as they often work on the fringes of the formal economy assisting their husbands with manual labor, or producing food to feed their families as opposed to food for sale.

In India there are over 258 million people working in the agricultural sector, and up to 70 percent of rural women are engaged in the agricultural workforce. There have been some noteworthy success stories in India around the creation of innovative technology solutions for agricultural workers. An Indian midwife, Arkhiben Vankar, became known as the pesticide lady when she developed an herbal pesticide that was efficient, low-cost, and toxin-free. This innovation provided Indian women engaged in agricultural work with an alternative to harmful chemical pesticides. Another technological innovation was designed by Subharani Kurian, who developed a bicycle-operated duplex pump to draw up ground water. The innovation assists women based on the idea that leg muscles are more powerful than hand muscles, making a bicycle pump more effective to operate.

Lack of communication, education, and access to technology among women, particularly in developing countries, has often prevented women from receiving the same benefits and opportunities as men in the agricultural sector. For the last 50 years, the United States Agency for International Development (USAID) has helped to bring scientific knowledge and technology to poor agricultural workers in developing countries through initiatives like the Collaborative Research Support Programs (CRSPs). According to USAID, "by empowering women farmers with the same access to land, new technologies and capital as men, we can increase crop yields by as much as 30 percent and feed an additional 150 million people."

Support Worker Advocacy Organizations

Research can be a useful tool to examine risks associated with the agricultural industry and how to mitigate them in the future, thus ensuring that vulnerable workers do not risk losing their livelihoods. Agriculture is one of the most dangerous industries to work in due to hazardous machinery, livestock, extreme weather conditions, dehydration, and exposure to pesticides.

In China there are an estimated 225 million agricultural workers, but farms are increasingly worked by the youngest and oldest residents of rural communities, as many middle-aged wage workers seek employment in cities. Injuries are abundant due to use of heavy machinery, and result in millions of deaths and disabilities among farmworkers each year. A collaborative research project between the Colorado Injury Control Research Center, the Center for Injury Research and Policy at The Ohio State University, and the Tongji Injury Control Research Center was undertaken between Chinese and American researchers to find solutions to reduce agriculturally related injuries in China. The program has trained over 80 researchers, published studies on agricultural injuries, and opened a center for injury prevention in China. The project aims to provide insights on how to train agricultural workers to safely handle new machinery to avoid future injuries and deaths.

The project aims to provide insights on how to train agricultural workers to safely handle new machinery to avoid future injuries and deaths.

Consumers can make a positive contribution towards the health care of farmworkers in the United States through non-profit organizations such as the National Center for Farmworker Health (NCFH). The organization is dedicated to improving worker health in the United States by providing services like resources for migrants, training programs, and education and policy analysis. The public can get involved through NCFH's Gift of Health program, which accepts donations that are invested in promoting the health of America's farmworkers.

Get Involved and Be Aware—Locally and Globally

Local initiatives that invest in the well-being of vulnerable communities can effectively help change the conditions of agricultural workers. Farmworkers are often described as hidden people, usually subjected to impoverished living conditions, with limited access to basic services like water and electricity.

South Africa's wine and fruit industry alone generates US $3 billion a year for the South African economy. Yet, according to a Human Rights Watch report, farmworkers benefit very little from the profits, and are often forced to live in substandard housing. Solms-Delta is an example of a South African wine estate that has established its own initiative, the Wijn de Caap Trust, to break the cycle of poverty among farmworkers on the Solms-Delta estate. The trust receives 33 percent of profits from the estate's wine sales, which aims to improve the lives of farmworkers by providing quality housing, investing in education facilities for children, and providing medical care to families.

Consumers in the United States can also become directly involved in community farming enterprises by volunteering or working at local farmers' markets, participating in volunteer days at nearby farms, or even apprenticing on a farm for a season. Visit https://attra.ncat.org/attra-pub/internships/ to learn more about on-farm opportunities in the United States and Canada.

Promote Universal Education

Education can be used from a grassroots level to dispel ignorance and empower local communities. Agricultural workers often migrate in search of seasonal or temporary work, and can be unaware of their rights due to poor education, isolation within rural areas, and fragmented organization. Education programs can also help inform consumers on ethical considerations of food production, and educate young leaders on policy formulation and advocacy.

Student Action with Farmworkers (SAF) is an innovative nonprofit organization, which uses popular education to raise awareness of issues around farmworker conditions in local US communities. SAF works with farmworkers, students and advocates alike, and has provided support to over 80,000 farmworkers to gain access to health, legal, and education facilities.

Vote With Your Dollar

Consumers can choose products produced in environmentally friendly and socially responsible ways. By purchasing products that are not linked to the exploitation of agricultural laborers, it sends the message to agricultural employers that consumers do not support abusive labor conditions, and that they are willing to pay an often-higher price for ethically produced goods. This helps ensure that workers are paid fairly and do not work under poor conditions.

Fair Trade USA is an international movement that allows customers to buy products from all over the world that support poverty-reduction projects, relieve exploitation, and endorse environmental sustainability. The Fair Trade standards enable agricultural workers to work in safe and inclusive environments, follow economic trade contracts with fair pricing, improve their own living conditions, and avoid child labor. There is growing demand from consumers for socially responsible food production; North America will soon implement its own Food Justice label. This label will also help lift American workers out of poverty by guaranteeing fair wages, adequate living conditions, and reasonable contracts.

Agriculture will not be viable while the vast majority of its workforce lives in poverty around the world, and innovative measures to break this cycle of poverty, along with your contributions, are crucial to fostering a healthier food system.

Agriculture Could Be Instrumental in Increasing Africa's Wealth

Akinwumi Adesina

Dr. Akinwumi Adesina is President of the African Development Bank. He has previously held the position of Vice President of Policy and Partnerships for the Alliance for a Green Revolution in Africa.

Agriculture is instrumental in Africa's poverty: it must also be instrumental in its wealth. Only through agricultural regeneration can growth, diversification and job creation occur for African economies, for no region of the world has ever industrialised without the agricultural sector being first transformed.

In short, the future of Africa depends on agriculture. But Africa cannot develop quickly if farming remains largely a subsistence activity. 60% of the population are involved in farming, yet it accounts for less than one seventh of its GDP, and African agricultural yield is the lowest in the world.

So Africa is late in developing but even this very fact offers a large scale opportunity for international investors and big-ticket entrepreneurs.

Economic diversification and lasting wealth creation begins with a vibrant agriculture sector. Between $30 and $40 billion a year over the next ten years is needed to transform African agriculture and create the vibrancy. It's a lot of money, but it is available, even within Africa, if the projects are good enough.

And they ought to be good enough, since such investments will create new markets worth at least $85 billion per year in added revenue by 2025. That's a potential return of at least 100%. But which producers will own, influence and leverage these markets? Most, surely, should be made in Africa? We must own our development.

"The Future of Africa Depends on Agriculture," by Dr. Akinwumi Adesina, President, African Development Bank Group, May 9, 2017. Reprinted by permission.

The commitments of last year's [African Green Revolution Forum] (AGRF) gave us a flying start with $30 billion over 10 years.

And with such transformation would come the reduction of Africa's net trade deficit in food, potentially bringing net savings of up to $100 billion per year. We must bring an end to the costly and damaging anomaly of the net deficit in food. No more should Africa produce what it does not or cannot consume, and no more should it consume what it does not (but could easily) produce.

Other related measures would deliver similarly impressive albeit incalculable financial impacts: fiscal inclusion, tax reform, domestic revenue mobilization, higher remittances, reduced corruption and better governance.

There are also still huge and unexploited growth opportunities in Africa. The continent is endowed with 65% of the world's uncultivated arable land and huge reserves of water. Sub Saharan Africa also has 10% of the world's oil reserves, 40% of its gold, and up to 90% of its chromium and platinum. And those are just the known reserves—the whole continent is one of the world's largest unexplored resource basins. Africa may suffer from poverty but it is an unimaginably rich continent, even after fifty years and more of commodity exploitation.

But how to bring about this transformation? How to close this potential deal of the century? Public and private sector should be acting together. They are needed to provide significant opportunities for Africa's emerging innovators and entrepreneurs, not to mention its financiers, fund managers and financial advisers.

Over the past few years, the Bank has been able to bring about a comprehensive re-evaluation of the potentially enormous role of agriculture in the transformation of Africa, and the AGRF has been a critical factor in the shared objective with the Bank of bringing about the green revolution in Africa.

The technologies to feed Africa exist already. This is the period of climate change. High yielding drought-tolerant maize can allow farmers to grow a good crop even during droughts. Some cassava varieties can yield 80 tonnes per hectare. High yielding rice varieties that meet or beat international standards of imported rice now exist. Orange-fleshed sweet potatoes allow us to address the problem of vitamin A deficiency. Tropical and drought-tolerant wheat varieties are being grown in Nigeria, Kenya and Sudan.

These technologies need to be scaled up for widespread adoption. This will not happen by itself. It will require specific incentives. In particular, the African Development Bank and the World Bank plan to jointly provide $800 million through "Technologies for African Agricultural Transformation," a flagship programme for the scaling up of agricultural technologies to reach millions of farmers in Africa over the next ten years.

For agricultural transformation more generally, the African Development Bank has committed $24 billion to agriculture over the next 10 years, with a sharp focus on food self-sufficiency and agro-industrialization.

It's also why we launched the Affirmative Finance Action for Women in Africa (AFAWA), to make an extra $3 billion available for women entrepreneurs, in order to improve food production levels on the basis that women are demonstrably more dependable and bankable than men.

Getting our youth involved in agriculture as a business is crucial. That is why the Bank launched the ENABLE Youth program. This program will provide access to capital and capacity to "Agripreneurs" to create about 300,000 agribusinesses and 1.5 million jobs in 30 countries across Africa, with an estimated investment of $15 billion over the next five years.

With so many entrepreneurs now on the case of farming, an issue to resolve quickly is the current low level of commercial financing for agriculture. Finance and farming have not been easy partners in Africa, and the farming sector receives less than 3% of the overall financing provided by the banking sector.

The African Development Bank is promoting national risk sharing facilities in every country to leverage agricultural finance, similar to the Nigeria Incentive-Based Risk Sharing for Agricultural Lending (NIRSAL), a facility designed to reduce the risks of lending to Nigerian agriculture value chains. The impact in Nigeria was massive. Over four years, 15 million farmers were reached, 2.5 million of them women. Food production expanded by over 21 million tonnes. Today, several African countries are adopting the approach, as well as others such as Afghanistan.

I predict that the next few years will see agriculture emerge fully from poverty and subsistence to become the next big booming business sector of Africa, with entrepreneurs, financiers, inventors and innovators all gathering round a honey pot of bankable projects, programmes and opportunities. After all, who eats copper? And who drinks oil? Africans need to become producers and creators, and not just consumers, in the fast-moving enterprising business of food.

The African Development Bank will play its active role as a catalyst of this activity, and I am confident that we will soon see Africa's first tranche of billionaires coming from the farming and food sectors.

The World Trade Organization Is to Blame for Inequality in Agriculture, Not Agribusinesses

Timothy A. Wise and Sophia Murphy

Timothy A. Wise is a senior researcher at the Small Planet Institute and Tufts University. Sophia Murphy is a senior advisor at the Institute for Agriculture and Trade Policy.

Farm leaders from around the world converged in Buenos Aires this week. They traveled to pressure the trade ministers attending the biennial World Trade Organization (WTO) Ministerial Conference to stop unfair trade practices that are hurting farmers. Once again, they went home empty-handed.

Some farmers lobbied delegates inside the heavily fortified Hilton Hotel, where the WTO trade ministers huddled for four days. More took to the streets, where their "Agriculture Out of the WTO!" banners waved in a week of peaceful protests.

The talks closed Wednesday evening with a whimper, as Director-General Roberto Azevêdo conceded that little progress had been made, and none on agricultural issues. Notably, and egregiously, US Trade Representative Robert Lighthizer refused to engage in promised negotiations on a permanent solution on the use of food reserves by India and other countries for food distribution systems. India and other developing countries would not make concessions on any area without resolution on this issue, and the talks ended without even a perfunctory formal declaration.

Neither farmers nor WTO member governments were expecting much from Buenos Aires. As it turned out, no expectation could have been low enough.

"Keep Your Eyes on the Price: WTO Remains Blind to Agricultural Dumping," by Timothy A. Wise and Sophia Murphy, Food Tank. Reprinted by permission.

The Return of Dumping

Lighthizer's open indifference to the concerns and priorities of other poorer member states is an insult to farmers and a threat to global food security. Agricultural prices have fallen from their 2008 peaks. Grain traders are again flooding international markets with surplus production grown in the United States and other agricultural export powers. Low-priced exports are a disaster for poor farmers, who see their crop prices dragged down to unsustainable levels in local markets.

Exporting a product at a price below what it cost to produce is one definition of dumping, an unfair trade practice that is supposed to be disciplined by the WTO. According to new research by the Institute for Agriculture and Trade Policy (IATP), in 2015 the US was exporting major agricultural commodities at dumping-level prices: corn at 12 percent below production costs, soybeans at 10 percent, cotton at 23 percent, and wheat at 32 percent. There is little indication that prices are likely to rise any time soon.

The food price spikes of 2008 brought new attention to the need for developing countries to reduce their dependence on imports and invest in their small-scale food producers. Many are doing that. African governments, for example, committed to raising their levels of agricultural development support to 10 percent of government budgets.

When those small-scale farmers start growing enough food to sell their surpluses on local markets, they need to get a decent price. When crop prices were high, many did, which put more money in the hands of rural people. Since 2014, however, the world has created what Reuters called a "global grain glut," driving down prices.

In such conditions, farmers desperately need protection from below-cost imports. They need structures that limit the risks they cannot control and to protect them from the highly concentrated market power of seed, farm input, and commodity trading companies. Many developing countries need active and engaged governments to build and develop stable and profitable markets for farmers.

First, Do No Harm

The WTO was established to provide a fair, rules-based, and transparent international trade system. Poor and irresponsible management of subsidized agricultural surpluses from Europe and the US plagued international markets in the 1980s. The WTO Agreement on Agriculture was meant to stop that. It is still the only institution that can credibly claim a mandate to do it, and the only trade agreement that seeks to discipline agricultural subsidies.

Yet the global grain glut was barely noted in the negotiations, even though it is precisely the kind of economic coordination a global trade body should engage in. Worse, the Buenos Aires summit refused to agree on a longstanding set of proposals from developing countries to help them protect themselves from dumping:

- Public stockholding—The US government has called out India and other developing countries for excessive subsidies to their farmers under ambitious government programs that pay support prices to farmers to build food reserves, which are then drawn upon to distribute to the poor. In India, that program is intended to reach 840 million people. The support price protects farmers from dumping-level prices. Despite a WTO commitment four years ago to resolve the issue in 2017, US negotiators nixed any agreement.
- Special Safeguard Mechanism—Rich countries already have the right to impose protective measures when imports surge and threaten prices for domestic producers. A proposal to allow developing countries the same rights has languished for years, and it was not even discussed in Buenos Aires.
- Relief for cotton farmers—Since 2004, the WTO has promised expedited action to reduce rich country subsidies to cotton producers—mainly in the US—that were found to

be in violation of WTO rules against dumping. Millions of small-scale farmers, in West Africa and elsewhere, depend on cotton for their livelihoods. Thirteen years later, they are still waiting for the WTO to act, as US negotiators continue to block actions that could reduce US cotton dumping.

- Reductions in trade-distorting domestic support—One of the stated goals of the current Doha Development Agenda, adopted in 2001, was to end rich country policies that harm importing countries. The issue has scarcely been mentioned since negotiations on it collapsed in 2008, and it got barely a mention in Buenos Aires.

Eyes on the Price

Does this diplomatic merry-go-round matter any more? Why would farm leaders expect this intergovernmental organization to resolve problems that the WTO agreements themselves have partly caused? An institution that was the pride of a generation of US government officials, together with the international companies they allied with, has today become a favored whipping post for President Donald Trump and his trade officials.

Without a commitment from the world's largest economy, it is very hard to see how the multilateral institution will function, at least in the short term. One year into his administration, Trump does not even have a confirmed WTO ambassador in place.

If the WTO is to fulfill its mandate to support development and reduce unfair trade, it has to keep its eyes on the prize of fair prices. In Buenos Aires, member governments instead put their heads in the sand.

What farmers and civil society organizations are after is accountability and congruence with multilateral obligations, especially the sustainable development goals. The multilateral trade system urgently needs to adapt if the world is to respond to the challenges of climate change, economic inequality, social exclusion, and the growing monopoly control of transnational firms across the food system.

There are enough rules telling countries what they may not do. It is time for trade rules that give countries a positive agenda to promote development and food security while protecting farmers from dumping.

Organizations to Contact

The editors have compiled the following list of organizations concerned with the issues debated in this book. The descriptions are derived from materials provided by the organizations. All have publications or information available for interested readers. This list was compiled on the date of publication of the present volume; the information provided here may change. Be aware that many organizations take several weeks or longer to respond to inquiries, so allow as much time as possible.

Action for Healthy Kids
600 West Van Buren St., Suite 720
Chicago, IL 60607
phone: (800) 416-5136
email: volunteer@actionforhealthykids.org
website: www.actionforhealthykids.org

Action for Healthy Kids focuses on childhood obesity. They are a grassroots organization committed to offering healthier options—from food to exercise—within public schools. They work with schools and advocate for better government policies.

Black Urban Growers
email: volunteers@blackfarmersconf.org
website: www.blackurbangrowers.org

Black Urban Growers (BUGS) is an organization that offers education on and advocacy for food and farm issues. They focus on black collective leadership, addressing the racial disparity in food justice initiatives. They also convene the Black Farmers & Urban Gardeners Conference.

The Earth Institute
Columbia University
Hogan Hall
2910 Broadway, Level A
New York, NY 10025
phone: (212) 854-3830
email: edufour@ei.columbia.edu
website: www.earth.columbia.edu

The Earth Institute is based at Columbia University in New York. They provide research and education with the goal of influencing public policy. Their focus is to create a more sustainable world.

The Ethical Farming Fund
phone: (412) 353-9744
email: info@ethicalfarmingfund.org
website: www.ethicalfarmingfund.org

The Ethical Farming Fund is a nonprofit focused on western Pennsylvania's food network. They promote ethical farming practices and support local farmers. Ethical farming's tenets include animal welfare; sustainability; organic meat, eggs, and dairy; transparency; and producing and buying local food.

Farm Forward
PO Box 4120
Portland, OR 97208
phone: (877) 313-3276
email: info@farmforward.com
website: www.farmforward.com

Farm Forward is an organization that promotes conscientious food choice, animal welfare on farms, and sustainable agriculture. They achieve these goals through educating consumers, supporting research and teaching at the collegiate level, and through outreach via films, books, and other organizations.

The Food Empowerment Project
PO Box 7322
Cotati, CA 94931
phone: (717) 779-8004
email: info@foodispower.org
website: www.foodispower.org

The Food Empowerment Project focuses on sustainability through food choice. They believe consumers can affect change by voting with their dollar. They provide information about what companies are sustainable and have fair worker policies. They are a vegan food justice organization and a nonprofit.

Johns Hopkins Center for a Livable Future
Johns Hopkins Bloomberg School of Public Health
111 Market Place, Suite 840
Baltimore, MD 21202
phone: (410) 223-1811
email: clf@jhsph.edu
website: www.jhsph.edu/research/centers-and-institutes/johns-hopkins-center-for-a-livable-future

The Center for a Livable Future provides research, educational tools, and advice on food system policies, food security, and the environmental costs of our food systems. Currently, their priorities include factory farming, food equity and access, food waste, and antibiotic resistance. The Center for a Livable Future is an offshoot of the Johns Hopkins Bloomberg School of Public Health.

Just Food
email: info@justfood.org
website: www.justfood.org

Just Food is a nonprofit located in New York City. They advocate for food justice and sustainable agriculture. They are also concerned with local communities and racial, social, economic, and environmental justice.

Monsanto Fund
800 N. Lindbergh Blvd.
St. Louis, MO 63167
website: www.monsantofund.org

The Monsanto Fund is an organization that fosters education, community development, and food and nutrition initiatives in farming communities. Monsanto is part of the Bayer Corporation, which counts agriculture as one of its main industries. The fund works primarily through partnering with other organizations and donating money.

New York City Community Garden Coalition
232 East 11th St.
New York, NY, 10003
phone: (347) 699-6099
website: www.nyccgc.org

The New York City Community Garden Coalition focuses on empowering community gardens throughout New York City. Community gardens are often tended by communities of color and provide both fresh food and a gathering place for said communities. The coalition seeks to preserve and create these gardens.

Organic Farming Research Foundation
303 Potrero St., Suite 29-203
Santa Cruz, CA 95060
phone: (831) 426-6606
email: info@ofrf.org
website: www.ofrf.org

The Organic Farming Research Foundation (OFRF) is a nonprofit that advocates for widespread organic farming. They have worked in cooperation with the United States Department of Agriculture. They provide grants to local farms and researchers as well as training on organic advocacy.

Polyface Farm
43 Pure Meadows Lane
Swoope, VA 24479
phone: (540) 885-3590
website: www.polyfacefarms.com

Polyface is a working organic farm. They are one of the best-known non-industrial food producers. They promote transparency through open farm visits, and sustainability through grass-based livestock and by avoiding monocultures. They also focus on their local community, refusing to ship food.

Rise & Root Farm
email: karen@riseandrootfarm.com
website: www.riseandrootfarm.com

Rise & Root Farm is a cooperatively run farm in Orange County, New York, that uses sustainable growing techniques. They hope to set an example for the public of what farming can be. Rise & Root Farm is helmed by women, teachers, people of color, students, and growers.

Slow Foods USA
1000 Dean St., Suite 402
Brooklyn, NY 11238
phone: (718) 260-8000
email: membership@slowfoodusa.org
website: www.slowfoodusa.org

Slow Food USA is an organization that functions both locally and globally. They advocate for clean food from the ground up. Their platform promotes sustainable practices, worker justice, local food, and nutrition.

Bibliography

Books

Cheryl J. Baldwin. *Sustainability in the Food Industry*. Hoboken, NJ: John Wiley & Sons, 2012.

Dan Barber. *The Third Plate: Field Notes on the Future of Food*. New York, NY: Penguin, 2014.

Natasha Bowens. *The Color of Food: Stories of Race, Resilience, and Farming*. Gabriola Island, BC: New Society Publishers, 2015.

Barry Estabrook. *Tomatoland: How Modern Industrial Agriculture Destroyed Our Most Alluring Fruit*. Kansas City, MO: Andrew McMeel Press, 2012.

Wenonah Hauter. *Foodopoly: The Battle Over the Future of Food and Farming in America*. New York, NY: The New Press, 2014.

Jonathan Kauffman. *Hippie Food: How Back-to-the-Landers, Longhairs, and Revolutionaries Changed the Way We Eat*. New York, NY: HarperCollins, 2018.

Megan Kimble. *Unprocessed: My City-Dwelling Year of Reclaiming Real Food*. New York, NY: William Morrow, 2015.

Kristin Lawless. *Formerly Known as Food: How the Industrial Food System is Changing Our Minds, Bodies, and Culture*. London, UK: St. Martin's Press, 2018.

Tracie McMillan. *The American Way of Eating: Undercover at Walmart, Applebee's, Farm Fields and the Dinner Table*. New York, NY: Scribner, 2012.

David R. Montgomery. *Growing a Revolution: Bringing Our Soil Back to Life*. New York, NY: WW Norton, 2018.

Michael Moss. *Salt Sugar Fat: How the Food Giants Hooked Us.* New York, NY: Random House, 2013.

Marion Nestle. *Food Politics: How the Food Industry Influences Nutrition and Health.* Berkeley, CA: University of California Press, 2013.

Brian K. Obach. *Organic Struggle: The Movement for Sustainable Agriculture in the United States.* Boston, MA: MIT Press, 2017.

Larry Olmsted. *Real Food/Fake Food: Why You Don't Know What You're Eating and What You Can Do About It.* Chapel Hill, NC: Algonquin Books, 2016.

Raj Patel. *Stuffed and Starved: The Hidden Battle for the World Food System,* Rev. Edition. New York, NY: Melville House, 2012.

Michael Ruhlman. *Grocery: The Buying and Selling of Food in America.* New York, NY: Abrams Books, 2017.

Ronald L. Sandler. *Food Ethics: The Basics.* London, UK: Routledge, 2014.

Mark Schatzker. *The Dorito Effect: The Surprising New Truth about Food and Flavor.* New York, NY: Simon & Schuster, 2016.

Eric Schlosser. *Fast Food Nation: The Dark Side of the All-American Meal.* Boston, MA: Mariner Books, 2012.

Ellen K. Silbergeld. *Chickenizing Farms and Food: How Industrial Meat Production Endangers Workers, Animals, and Consumers.* Baltimore, MD: Johns Hopkins University Press, 2016.

Periodicals and Internet Sources

Julie Beck, "Preventing Food Poisoning in the Age of a Globalized Food Supply," *Atlantic*, June 26, 2015. https://www.theatlantic.com/health/archive/2015/06/preventing

-food-poisoning-in-the-age-of-a-globalized-food-supply /396920/.

Joanna Blythman, "Inside the Food Industry: The Surprising Truth about What You Eat," *Guardian*, February 21, 2015. https://www.theguardian.com/lifeandstyle/2015/feb/21/a -feast-of-engineering-whats-really-in-your-food.

Cody Carlson, "The Ag Gag Laws: Hiding Factory Farm Abuses from Public Scrutiny," *Atlantic*, March 20, 2012. https://www.theatlantic.com/health/archive/2012/03 /the-ag-gag-laws-hiding-factory-farm-abuses-from-public -scrutiny/254674/.

Adam Chandler, "Why Americans Lead the World in Food Waste," *Atlantic*, July 15, 2016. https://www.theatlantic.com /business/archive/2016/07/american-food-waste/491513/.

Diana Donlon, "The Agricultural Fulcrum: Better Food, Better Climate," *Atlantic*, January 18, 2013. https://www .theatlantic.com/health/archive/2013/01/the-agricultural -fulcrum-better-food-better-climate/267298/.

Daniel Engber, "Dark Sugar: The Decline and Fall of High-Fructose Corn Syrup," *Slate*, April 28, 2009. https:// slate.com/technology/2009/04/the-decline-and-fall -of-high-fructose-corn-syrup.html.

Andrea Gantaz, "'Big Organic' Growth has Agriculture at Crossroads," *WATTAgNet*, April 2, 2018. https://www .wattagnet.com/articles/33967-big-organic-growth-has -agriculture-at-crossroads.

Danny Hakim, "At Hamburger Central, Antibiotics for Cattle that Aren't Sick," *New York Times*, March 23, 2018. https:// www.nytimes.com/2018/03/23/business/cattle-antiobiotics .html?rref=collection%2Ftimestopic%2FFactory%20 Farming&action=click&contentCollection=timestopics &region=stream&module=stream_unit&version =latest&contentPlacement=7&pgtype=collection.

James Hamblin, "How Agriculture Controls Nutrition Guidelines," *Atlantic*, October 8, 2015. https://www .theatlantic.com/health/archive/2015/10/ag-v-nutrition /409390/.

James Hamblin, "The US is Not Eating and Wasting Twice as Much Food as It Did in 1975," *Atlantic*, August 30, 2016. https://www.theatlantic.com/health/archive/2016/08/twice -as-much-food-as-1975/497939/.

James McWilliams, "Meat: What Big Agriculture and the Ethical Butcher Have in Common," *Atlantic*, February 8, 2012. https://www.theatlantic.com/health/archive/2012/02 /meat-what-big-agriculture-and-the-ethical-butcher-have -in-common/252679/.

Monica Reinagel, "Pesticides on Our Plates: Is Our Food Safe to Eat?" *Scientific American*, January 19, 2019. https:// www.scientificamerican.com/article/pesticides-on-our -plates-is-our-food-safe-to-eat/.

Lisa Schmesier, "Technological Revolution Set to Hit Farmers— If They Can Afford It," *Observer*, July 28, 2017. https:// observer.com/2017/07/technology-automation-farming -labor-shortage/.

Bibi Van der Zee, "Why Factory Farming is Not Just Cruel—But Also a Threat to All Life on the Planet," *Guardian*, October 4, 2017. https://www.theguardian.com/environment/2017 /oct/04/factory-farming-destructive-wasteful-cruel-says -philip-lymbery-farmageddon-author.

Sophie Yeo, "Agriculture is a Big Climate Problem. Now Farmers Are Sharing Solutions," *Grist*, December 18, 2018. https://grist.org/article/agriculture-climate-change-cop24 -katowice-soil-carbon/.

Index